MW00815267

THE ENERGY NUMBER BOOK

By MARIE DIAMOND

*Feng Shui Master
and Master Teacher in the
Global Phenomena "The Secret"*

Copyright and Published by Marie Diamond Publishing

www.MarieDiamond.com

Copyright Malibu, California, USA, 2023

Published in the USA

By Marie Diamond Publishing

www.MarieDiamond.com

Content Copyright © Marie Diamond, 2023

Illustrations Copyright © Marie Diamond, 2023

All rights reserved. No portion of this book may be reproduced, stored in a retrieval system or transmitted at any time or by any means mechanical, electronic, photocopying, recording or otherwise, without the prior, written permission of the publisher. The Right of Marie Diamond to be identified as the author of this work has been asserted by Californian Laws.

www.MarieDiamond.com

ISBN 979-8-9878335-0-6

Welcome to The Energy Number Book.

I wrote this book to support you in your personal transformation. It will help you to better understand yourself, and the lessons you need to learn in regard to your Success, Health, Relationships, and Wisdom.

You will learn new tools that will help you change your Personal Law of Attraction. These tools will not only change the way you will live your life but how you connect with God and the Universe. You'll learn what kind of careers would work best for you, what health advice you need to pay attention to, how best to enhance your relationships, and which wisdom practices will give you the best results.

The Energy Number Book will teach you about how to use your Personal Energy Number to manifest your dreams faster and more effortlessly. You'll learn all about your best directions based on your personal energy. In Diamond Feng Shui, location is everything. Being in the right place can change your life!

You'll be able to find your Personal Energy Number in the pages of this book, and you can also find it on the Marie Diamond app. Simply head to the app and enter in your details to learn your Personal Energy Number, archetype, and your four best directions according to Feng Shui.

For iPhones, go to:
https://apps.apple.com/us/app/marie-diamond/id971250423

For Android phones, go to:
https://play.google.com/store/apps/details?id=com.mariediamond.magicalliving

Thank you for joining me on this exciting journey of transformation.

With Love,
Marie Diamond
www.MarieDiamond.com

SOCIAL MEDIA
Follow Me on Facebook: @MarieDiamondFans
Follow Me on Instagram: @Mariediamond8
Check Out My YouTube Channel: @MarieDiamond
For Spanish-Speaking Students:
Go to www.MarieDiamondEspanol.com

CONTENT

The Energy Number Book

INTRODUCTION

When I first started studying Feng Shui many years ago, I soon realized just how important a role your home environment plays in the Law of Attraction.

Diamond Feng Shui is my own unique system that uses traditional Feng Shui teachings and combines them with the Law of Attraction, neuroscience, and quantum physics principles. Put simply, Diamond Feng Shui turns your home into a three-dimensional vision board! It teaches you how to use each room in your home, be it a studio apartment or a five-bedroom house, in order to increase the good energy, and improve your life.

In Diamond Feng Shui, there is the belief that each person's fortune is the sum of three different kinds of, but equally important, luck – Heaven Luck, Human Luck, and Earth Luck.

Heaven Luck refers to the life circumstances you were born into - your family, culture, your physical abilities, and so on. These tend to be fixed conditions that can't easily be changed. Some view this as the path that God has chosen for you, or refer to it as your destiny or karma.

Human Luck refers to your attitude, behavior, and the choices you make every day that affect your life. It's the focus of most self-help books; the idea that changing your attitude will change your life. It goes without saying that a positive and grateful attitude are important, but it requires a lot of time, practice, and discipline to learn to think that way.

Luckily, Earth Luck is the easiest and quickest to improve; all it takes is some basic knowledge and a little elbow grease. Earth Luck refers to changing your environment to improve the good "chi" around you. It stands to reason that if your home is in chaos with clutter, dust, broken objects and dimly lit rooms, it's harder to attract positive energy into your life. Similarly, if your house is closed up and unwelcoming, how can you expect good things to find you?

In addition to the three different kinds of luck, Diamond Feng Shui states that there isn't a singular, one-size-fits-all approach. Since everybody is different, it makes sense that the energy flows differently for them in their home. For this reason, Diamond Feng Shui takes into account something called your Personal Energy Number.

This way this number is calculated is very different from traditional numerology. Your Personal Energy Number is a number from one to nine and is based on your date of birth and the gender you were assigned with at birth.

Each Energy Number represents a different archetype - similar to how each different horoscope comes with a different set of personality traits. Your Energy Number will also tell you your four best compass directions where the energy in each room in your home is the most powerful for you. There's the best direction for attracting success, good health, good relationships, and wisdom and personal growth.

By taking your Personal Energy Number into account, you end up with a much more personalized, and ultimately more powerful, Feng Shui system. You'll be able to direct this energy, or chi, to attract the things you want in life by doing something as simple as facing a different direction when we sleep, or when we sit at our desks.

The Marie Diamond App

Discover your Personal Energy Number and your four best Feng Shui directions to create a more abundant and successful life. Start your very own and interactive Energy Number Journey with personalized meditations, affirmations, and Feng Shui activations. Available now for both Androids and iPhones.

Personal Energy Number Archetypes

Energy Number 1	The Wealth Creator
Energy Number 2	The Teacher
Energy Number 3	The Bringer of Light
Energy Number 4	The Manager
Energy Number 5 (Man)	The Teacher
Energy Number 5 (Woman)	The Connector
Energy Number 6	The Creator
Energy Number 7	The Advisor
Energy Number 8	The Connector
Energy Number 9	The Healer

Personal Energy Number Chart

If you don't have access to a smartphone, no need to worry! Just locate your birthday on the chart to find your Personal Energy Number.

Year	Birthday	MAN	WOMAN
1921:	Feb 8, 1921 – Jan 27, 1922	7	8
1922:	Jan 28, 1922 – Feb 15, 1923	6	9
1923:	Feb 16, 1923 – Feb 4, 1924	5	1
1924:	Feb 5, 1924 – Jan 23, 1925	4	2
1925:	Jan 24, 1925 – Feb 12, 1926	3	2
1926:	Feb 13, 1926 – Feb 1, 1927	2	4
1927:	Feb 2, 1927 – Jan 22, 1928	1	5
1928:	Jan 23, 1928 – Feb 9, 1929	9	6
1929:	Feb 10, 1929 – Jan 29, 1930	8	7
1930:	Jan 30, 1930 – Feb 16, 1931	7	8
1931:	Feb 17, 1931 – Feb 5, 1932	6	9
1932:	Feb 6, 1932 – Jan 25, 1933	5	1
1933:	Jan 26, 1933 – Feb 13, 1934	4	2
1934:	Feb 14, 1934 – Feb 3, 1935	3	3
1935:	Feb 4, 1935 – Jan 23, 1936	2	4
1936:	Jan 24, 1936 – Feb 10, 1937	1	5

1937: Feb 11, 1937 – Jan 30, 1938	9	6
1938: Jan 31, 1938 – Feb 18, 1939	8	7
1939: Feb 19, 1939 – Feb 7, 1940	7	8
1940: Feb 8, 1940 – Jan 26, 1941	6	9
1941: Jan 27, 1941 – Feb 14, 1942	5	1
1942: Feb 15, 1942 – Feb 4, 1943	4	2
1943: Feb 5, 1943 – Jan 24, 1944	3	3
1944: Jan 25, 1944 – Feb 12, 1945	2	4
1945: Feb 13, 1945 – Feb 1, 1946	1	5
1946: Feb 2, 1946 – Jan 21, 1947	9	6
1947: Jan 22, 1947 – Feb 9, 1948	8	7
1948: Feb 10, 1948 – Jan 28, 1949	7	8
1949: Jan 29, 1949 – Feb 16, 1950	6	9
1950: Feb 17, 1950 – Feb 5, 1951	5	1
1951: Feb 6, 1951 – Jan 26, 1952	4	2
1952: Jan 27, 1952 – Feb 13, 1953	3	3
1953: Feb 14, 1953 – Feb 2, 1954	2	4
1954: Feb 3, 1954 – Jan 23, 1955	1	5
1955: Jan 24, 1955 – Feb 11, 1956	9	6
1956: Feb 12, 1956 – Jan 30, 1957	8	7

1957: Jan 31, 1957 – Feb 17, 1958	7	8
1958: Feb 18, 1958 – Feb 7, 1959	6	9
1959: Feb 8, 1959 – Jan 27, 1960	5	1
1960: Jan 28, 1960 – Feb 14, 1961	4	2
1961: Feb 15, 1961 – Feb 4, 1962	3	3
1962: Feb 5, 1962 – Jan 24, 1963	2	4
1963: Jan 25, 1963 – Feb 12, 1964	1	5
1964: Feb 13, 1964 – Feb 1, 1965	9	6
1965: Feb 2, 1965 – Jan 20, 1966	8	7
1966: Jan 21, 1966 – Feb 8, 1967	7	8
1967: Feb 9, 1967 – Jan 29, 1968	6	9
1968: Jan 30, 1968 – Feb 16, 1969	5	1
1969: Feb 17, 1969 – Feb 5, 1970	4	2
1970: Feb 6, 1970 – Jan 26, 1971	3	3
1971: Jan 27, 1971 – Feb 14, 1972	2	4
1972: Feb 15, 1972 – Feb 2, 1973	1	5
1973: Feb 3, 1973 – Jan 22, 1974	9	6
1974: Jan 23, 1974 – Feb 10, 1975	8	7
1975: Feb 11, 1975 – Jan 30, 1976	7	8
1976: Jan 31, 1976 – Feb 17, 1977	6	9

1977:	Feb 18, 1977 – Feb 6, 1978	5	1
1978:	Feb 7, 1978 – Jan 27, 1979	4	2
1979:	Jan 28, 1979 – Feb 15, 1980	3	3
1980:	Feb 16, 1980 – Feb 4, 1981	2	4
1981:	Feb 5, 1981 – Jan 24, 1982	1	5
1982:	Jan 25, 1982 – Feb 12, 1983	9	6
1983:	Feb 13, 1983 – Feb 1, 1984	8	7
1984:	Feb 2, 1984 – Feb 19, 1985	7	8
1985:	Feb 20, 1985 – Feb 8, 1986	6	9
1986:	Feb 9, 1986 – Jan 28, 1987	5	1
1987:	Jan 29, 1987 – Feb 16, 1988	4	2
1988:	Feb 17, 1988 – Feb 5, 1989	3	3
1989:	Feb 6, 1989 – Jan 26, 1990	2	4
1990:	Jan 27, 1990 – Feb 14, 1991	1	5
1991:	Feb 15, 1991 – Feb 3, 1992	9	6
1992:	Feb 4, 1992 – Jan 22, 1993	8	7
1993:	Jan 23, 1993 – Feb 9, 1994	7	8
1994:	Feb 10, 1994 – Jan 30, 1995	6	9
1995:	Jan 31, 1995 – Feb 18, 1996	5	1
1996:	Feb 19, 1996 – Feb 6, 1997	4	2

1997: Feb 7, 1997 – Jan 27, 1998	3	3
1998: Jan 28, 1998 – Feb 15, 1999	2	4
1999: Feb 16, 1999 – Feb 4, 2000	1	5
2000: Feb 5, 2000 – Jan 23, 2001	9	6
2001: Jan 24, 2001 – Feb 11, 2002	8	7
2002: Feb 12, 2002 – Jan 31, 2003	7	8
2003: Feb 1, 2003 – Jan 21, 2004	6	9
2004: Jan 22, 2004 – Feb 8, 2005	5	1
2005: Feb 9, 2005 – Jan 28, 2006	4	2
2006: Jan 29, 2006 – Feb 17, 2007	3	3
2007: Feb 18, 2007 – Feb 6, 2008	2	4
2008: Feb 7, 2008 – Jan 25, 2009	1	5
2009: Jan 26, 2009 – Feb 13, 2010	9	6
2010: Feb 14, 2010 – Feb 2, 201	8	7
2011: Feb 3, 2011 – Jan 22, 2012	7	8
2012: Jan 23, 2012 – Feb 9, 2013	6	9
2013: Feb10, 2013 – Jan 30, 2014	5	1
2014: Jan 31, 2014 – Feb 18, 2015	4	2
2015: Feb 19, 2015 – Feb 7, 2016	3	3
2016: Feb 8, 2016 – Jan 27, 2017	2	4

2017:	Jan. 28, 2017 – Feb 15, 2018	1	5
2018:	Feb. 16, 2018 – Feb 4, 2019	9	6
2019:	Feb. 5, 2019 – Jan 24, 2020	8	7
2020:	Jan. 25, 2020 – Feb 11, 2021	7	8
2021:	Feb 11, 2021 – Jan 31, 2022	6	9
2022:	Feb 1, 2022 – Jan 21, 2023	5	1
2023:	Jan 22, 2023 – Feb 09, 2024	4	2
2024:	Feb 10, 2024 – Jan 28, 2025	3	3

CHAPTER 1
Energy Number 1:
The Wealth Creator

Introduction

The Energy Archetype connected with Energy Number 1 is called the **Wealth Creator.** The essence of the Wealth Creator is:

"You seek, bring, and find fortune to all of the projects in your life, for yourself and for others. Money will be a gift to you. Being with your family will bring you peace. In your search for recognition, start stimulating your self-esteem. Your spiritual journey is a journey of reflection."

Famous People With This Energy Number:

Andy Warhol, Elizabeth Taylor, Dwayne "The Rock" Johnson, and Florence Pugh

Your Best Direction for <u>Success</u> is <u>Southeast</u>

1/ Soul Journey of Success

The Soul of Energy Number 1 has come to this planet to learn the Law of Abundance. At the end of their journey in this life, this Soul will understand that money is a reality they can create regardless of their family background. Wealth and riches are part of the beauty of the Universe.

You will see many artists with this number becoming very wealthy because they kept focusing on the abundance of their art. Wealth means that we can have it all. There are no limitations in wealth and you need to let go of the belief that your family background is an obstacle. Since you are the Universe, you can create financial abundance for yourself, your family and share it with your community and the world.

2/ Goals for Success

Affirmations share with the Universe your intention for what it is you want to accomplish in your life. But it's not just a message. There's strength in writing these goals in the present tense; you're not demanding or requesting. You're simply telling the Universe what will be. You should never write your affirmations in the future tense as there is great power in stating "This is the way I want my life to be, here and now".

Write down your Success goals on index cards, or place them on your vision board. You can also place them in the Southeast area of your living room, your bedroom, and your office.

Each goal sends your wishes to the Universe, and according to the Law of Attraction, you can attract anything you wish for. Just state your intentions and open yourself up to receive; let the Universe take care of the rest.

If you feel you don't want to place your goals out in the open, you can place them in nice, colored envelopes and address the front to the Universe, God, the Angels, or whomever you are praying to. Remember, Feng Shui is not connected with any specific religion. Instead, it respects all religions and belief systems.

Make your personal Success goals even more powerful by adding:

- An image that represents your goal
- An image of someone (such as a celebrity or someone you know personally) who has already attained a similar goal
- Any symbol that represents your goal

For Example:

You want to become successful in your business and bring good luck to your employees. You can add images of well-known people throughout history who have already accomplished this goal such as Henry Ford in the automobile industry. You can add images of money, such as a fake million-dollar bill, or photos of whatever it is you wish to have when you're a millionaire: a large mansion, a private jet, a yacht, or a gold watch.

3/ Quantum Colors for Success

In the Quantum Field, the colors for Success for the Energy Number 1 are **violet, lilac,** and **gold.** By placing these colors in the Southeast area of your home and office, you are sending a strong signal to the Universe to activate your Success. These colors were revealed to me after years of meditation and contemplation, and they are unique to Diamond Feng Shui.

4/ Professional Choices

For you, success and wealth are more likely when you choose the following activities or professional fields:

- Banker, investor, accountant, or financial advisor
- Fortune-seeker, diamond cutter, or collector
- Author of books on wealth and money
- Pastor or minister, ministry or foundation supporter
- Philanthropist, coach, or speaker helping others create wealth
- Sailor or boat maker
- Gold-seeker, jewelry maker, or watch maker
- Art dealer in very expensive art, deluxe products, or cars

5/ Feng Shui Activations For Your Success in your Home and Office

1. Facing Direction

During the day, make sure you're facing your Success direction (Southeast) whilst working or meeting up with clients. It's from the Southeast that your strongest Success energy flows. Your ability to attract Success increases greatly when you face towards the Southeast direction whilst you're working, sitting at your desk, looking at your computer screen, when meeting with people, negotiating, and signing contracts.

Avoid sitting with your back to the door since it's poor Feng Shui. From an evolutionary standpoint, our early ancestors faced a lot of dangers in their lives. From wild animals to attacks from other tribes, they had to be completely aware of their surroundings in order to survive. So, from that viewpoint, it makes sense to have a clear view of your door when you're sitting down or in bed so that you know exactly who's coming into the room. If you can't see the door, you make yourself vulnerable to people sneaking up on you. In terms of Feng Shui, you want to make sure you're in the path of the incoming flow of positive energy. You want to see all the good opportunities that enter through the door, and you want to make sure you're making yourself accessible to any good fortune that comes knocking.

2. Activate Your Personal Success Direction: Southeast

To attract great Success, you need to activate the Southeast area in three places:

- Professional success is focused in the Southeast area of your office

- Personal success is focused in the Southeast area of your living room or family room
- Romantic success is focused in the Southeast area of your bedroom

You can use a compass to find the correct direction. Southeast is between 112.5 and 157.5 degrees on a compass. Make sure you are standing facing the foot end of the bed or couch, or sitting down at your desk when you hold the compass. Similarly, you can use the Diamond Compass on the Marie Diamond app that is connected with your Personal Energy Number.

Next, examine the Southeast area of your office, living room, and bedroom. Do the items, furniture, paintings, and colors represent what you wrote down for your Success goals?

For example, if you have a vase with dead flowers, does this represent a blooming, blossoming career? Make sure there aren't any garbage cans or clutter in the Southeast area because they can block the flow of energy and symbolically put your Success "straight into the garbage".

Use objects that you already have in your home to activate your Success direction. Listed below are several options that will bring good chi to your Success energy:

- Cylinder-shaped objects, stripy objects, and long and tall objects

- Objects made out of wood, or images of flowers and plants (but no plants with spiky leaves like cactus, palm trees, or yuccas, because they create attacking energy in your living space)
- Real flowers and plants (again, no spiky leaves because they pick away at your success. You can also use silk flowers and plastic plants, but not dried flowers or plants)
- Brown, beige, green, or lilac-colored objects
- Magazines and books on financial advice or on creating wealth and money
- A wealth ship, a money frog, or a bowl with coins
- Images or books about millionaires and billionaires
- Items that are grouped together in fours (like four bamboo sticks bundled together)
- A little bubbling fountain
- An image of a small waterfall, or a river in a green lush landscape
- An image of fish swimming

In your office, you can also make the space more personal by placing any of the following in your Success direction:

- The logo of your company
- Your products or designs
- Your vision board with your goals
- A personal success affirmation card
- The royal blue Yin Yang symbol

Your Best Direction for <u>Health</u> is <u>East</u>

1/ Soul Journey of Health

In order for Energy Number 1 to have great health, you need to stay in touch with nature, just like how a child would. Longevity for an Energy Number 1 is more likely if you connect with nature on a regular basis.

Eat healthy food like salads, raw fruits, vegetables, and juices to activate your health. Take care of your feet and give them some air by walking barefoot in the fresh grass. Take long walks in the forest and enjoy the butterflies and the birds. Open yourself to eastern medicine and partake in exercises like Tai Chi and Qi Gong.

2/ Goals for Health

Write down your Health goals on index cards, or place them on your vision board. You can also place them in the East area of your living room, your bedroom, and your office.

Each goal sends your wishes to the Universe, and according to the Law of Attraction, you can attract anything you wish for. Just state your intentions and open yourself up to receive; let the Universe take care of the rest.

If you feel you don't want to place your goals out in the open, you can place them in nice, colored envelopes and address the front to the Universe, God, the Angels, or whomever you are praying to. Remember, Feng Shui is not connected with any specific religion. Instead, it respects all religions and belief systems.

Make your personal Health goals even more powerful by adding:

- An image that represents your goal
- An image of someone (such as a celebrity or someone you know personally) who has already attained a similar goal
- Any symbol that represents your goal

For Example:

You want to run a marathon. Add images of people running the New York Marathon. Add the date and your running time for completing the marathon.

3/ Quantum Colors for Health

In the Quantum Field, the colors for Health for the Energy number 1 are **emerald green, citrus green** and **iris blue**. By placing these colors in the East area of your home and office, you are sending a strong signal to the Universe to activate your Health.

4/ Health Practices

The following suggestions can help enhance your health energy. These suggestions will not guarantee your health, but instead will make it easier for you to become healthier:

- Always eat fresh foods and, if possible, eat organic produce
- Eat food that is in season
- Walk in nature, especially in the woods or forest, to stimulate your immune system
- Have a pedicure and let your feet be massaged
- Stimulate your health with the colors brown, green, blue, and black
- Learn to channel your chi by doing tai chi and Qi Gong exercises
- Make your body flexible with yoga
- Forgive yourself
- Remove clutter from your life
- Place an image of a dragon in your health direction
- Receive acupuncture treatments

5/ Feng Shui Activations For Your Health in Your Home and Office

1. Facing Direction

When you're in bed, sleep with the top of your head pointing toward your Health direction (East). During the day, sit in your living space or in your dining room facing your health direction.

Your energy level will increase when you sleep with the crown of your head pointing toward this direction, so arrange your bed so you can do so. If you lie on your couch when you're ill, make sure the top of your head faces the East.

2. Activate Your Personal Health Direction: East

To attract good Health, you need to activate the East in three places:

- To stimulate your energy for health when you're working, place Feng Shui activations in the East area of your office. A healthy worker creates a healthy business
- Place Feng Shui activations in the East of your living or family room so that during the daytime, you're creating good energy.
- Place Feng Shui activations in the East of your bedroom to stimulate your health whilst you're sleeping and to help you wake up energized in the morning

You can use a compass to find the correct direction. East is between 67.5 and 112.5 degrees on a compass. Make sure you are standing facing the foot end of the bed or couch, or sitting down at your desk when you hold the compass. Similarly, you can use the Diamond Compass on the Marie Diamond app that is connected with your Personal Energy Number.

Next, examine the East area of your office, living room, or bedroom. Do the items, furniture, paintings, and colors represent what you wrote down for your Health goals?

For example, an image of a cactus could attract a poor immune system, so it may not reflect the message you want to send to the Universe. Make sure there aren't any garbage cans or clutter in the East area because they can block the flow of energy and symbolically put your health "straight into the garbage".

Use objects that you already have in your home to activate your Health direction. Listed below are several options that will bring good chi to your Health energy:

- Long and tall objects, and objects with stripes
- Wooden or glass objects
- Antiques
- Flowers and plants, or images of flowers, plants, forests, or gardens
- Brown and green objects
- Pictures of your elders
- Pictures of the springtime
- An image of a river or a fountain
- Bamboo wind chimes

You can also make the space more personal by placing any of the following in your Health direction:

- An image of yourself when you appeared radiant and healthy in your living room
- Your vitamins, food supplements, workout or exercise equipment in your bedroom
- Books on health, yoga or relaxation in your office

Your Best Direction for <u>Relationships</u> is <u>South</u>

1/ Soul Journey of Relationships

As someone with an Energy Number 1, you need to allow the beautiful expression of who you are to become visible to the world. You can't hide anymore. You are creative and expressive, with a warm personality. Don't let your fears, doubts, and a lack of self-esteem cloud your mind. Perhaps you have attracted some friends, partners, or teachers in the past who were not supportive of your talents. Your fear of being visible attracted them into your life in order to gently push your soul to express itself to the world. You need to shine.

It's important that you show respect and recognition to your friends and family. Prioritize passion and celebration in your romantic relationships. Dance together, celebrate your anniversaries, have candlelit dinners, and treat your beloved to surprise gifts.

2/ Goals for Relationships

Write down your Relationship goals on index cards, or place them on your vision board. You can also place them in the South area of your living room, your bedroom, and your office.

Each goal sends your wishes to the Universe, and according to the Law of Attraction, you can attract anything you wish for. Just state your intentions and open yourself up to receive; let the Universe take care of the rest.

If you feel you don't want to place your goals out in the open, you can place them in nice, colored envelopes and address the front to the Universe, God, the Angels, or whomever you are praying to. Remember, Feng Shui is not connected with any specific religion. Instead, it respects all religions and belief systems.

Make your personal Relationship goals even more powerful by adding:

- An image that represents your goal
- An image of someone (such as a celebrity or someone you know personally) who has already attained a similar goal
- Any symbol that represents your goal

For Example:

You want to learn to tango with your romantic partner. Add images of people dancing the tango, or include sheet music of tango music.

Special Tip

Single women who want to have a steady romantic relationship should place peonies in their personal relationship direction. They can be real, silk, or just an image. Once you have attracted the relationship you wished for, give the peonies to someone who wishes to have the same kind of luck. Don't keep them. Men can do the same thing but use a bamboo plant instead of peonies.

3/ Quantum Colors for Relationships

In the Quantum Field, the colors for Relationships for Energy Number 1 are **ruby red**, **cherry red**, and **orange**. By placing these colors in the South area of your home and office, you are sending a strong signal to the Universe to activate your Relationships.

4/ Relationship Practices

The following are characteristic of those with an Energy Number of 1:

- You need to feel recognized and respected in your relationships

- You like to create music with others
- You love to party and celebrate
- You've had relationships with musicians, artists, and performers
- You love candlelight dinners and sitting around the fireplace with your family, drinking a glass of wine
- You like burning candles to make your home more welcoming to others
- The colors that stimulate your relationships are rose, pink, fuchsia, yellow, orange, and fire colors like red. Wood colors such as brown and green are also very stimulating
- You express your love with music and would enjoy playing a ballad at your partner's balcony
- You enjoy taking your date to the opera or concerts
- You like to set off fireworks for your family parties
- You like the idea of having a relationship with or falling in love with a celebrity

5/ Feng Shui Activations For Your Relationships in Your Home and Office

1. Facing Direction

Make sure you sit facing, or sleep with your head pointing towards your Relationship direction (South) in order to attract good relationships.

During the day, face the South when you're in the office, attending business meetings, dinners, or important conferences and you will be much more successful with your business relationships.

2. Activate Your Personal Relationship Direction: South

To attract better relationships, activate the South area in three places:

- For excellent professional relationships, focus on the South area of your office
- For family relationships, focus on the South area of your family or living room
- To stimulate your personal relationship, focus on the South area of your bedroom

You can use a compass to find the correct direction. South is between 157.5 and 202.5 degrees on a compass. Make sure you are standing facing the foot end of the bed or couch, or sitting down at your desk when you hold the compass. Similarly, you can use the Diamond Compass on the Marie Diamond app that is connected with your Personal Energy Number.

Next, examine the South area of your office, living room, or bedroom. Do the items, furniture, paintings, and colors represent what you wrote down for your Relationship goals?

For example, is an image of someone dancing alone in the rain representative of passion in your relationship? Make sure there aren't any garbage cans or clutter in the South area because they can block the flow of energy and symbolically put romance and passion "straight into the garbage".

Use objects that you already have in your home to activate your Relationship direction. Listed below are several options that will bring good chi to your Relationship energy:

- Triangle or pyramid-shaped objects, objects with stripes, or long and tall objects
- Objects made out of plastic or wood
- Images of flowers and plants (your plants should not have spiky leaves such as cactus, palm trees, or yuccas because they create attacking energy in your living space)
- Real flowers and plants (Again, don't use plants with spiky leaves because they pick away at your success)
- Silk flowers and plastic plants (but not dried flowers or plants)
- Fire colors such as red, purple, yellow, orange, rose, fuchsia, and brown
- Magazines and books about show business, art, music, or performance
- Red candles or a red lamp
- Images of famous musicians, dancers, and singers

You can also make the space more personal by placing any of the following in your Relationship direction:

- In your office, display a photo of your professional team, or of you and your manager. Also, place your address book or business cards from your clients in the South area
- In your living or family room, display recent photos of you with your loved ones. Also, photos of you and your friends
- In your bedroom, place photos of you with your romantic partner. Photos of you with your children can work here too, but not of you with your mother-in-law

Your Best Direction for <u>Wisdom</u> is <u>North</u>

1/ Soul Journey of Wisdom

As an Energy Number 1, you need to study alone without other people around you. It's better for you to reflect and contemplate alone. Take your fishing equipment, go sailing, or canoeing alone on the lake. Even hiking alone in the mountains will inspire you to be closer to God or the Universe.

The lesson you need to learn is to accept that this is the way you gather information, and the way you connect with your inner self. With that in mind, you still need to share your insights with others afterwards and understand that you need to be honest about how you find your wisdom.

You need to spend time by yourself in order to find peace and harmony. Taking a retreat on a regular basis will help you to tap into your intuition. Enlightenment is your ultimate goal in life.

For you, the journey is more important than the destination. You look up to the people that have done the journey before you.

2/ Goals for Wisdom

Write down your Wisdom goals on index cards, or place them on your vision board. You can also place them in the North area of your living room, your bedroom, and your office.

Each goal sends your wishes to the Universe, and according to the Law of Attraction, you can attract anything you wish for. Just state your intentions and open yourself up to receive; let the Universe take care of the rest.

If you feel you don't want to place your goals out in the open, you can place them in nice, colored envelopes and address the front to the Universe, God, the Angels, or whomever you are praying to. Remember, Feng Shui is not connected with any specific religion. Instead, it respects all religions and belief systems.

Make your personal Wisdom goals even more powerful by adding:

- An image that represents your goal
- An image of someone (such as a celebrity or someone you know personally) who has already attained a similar goal
- Any symbol that represents your goal

For Example:

You want to go on a pilgrimage. Add images of someone who is on a pilgrim and add a picture of the endpoint of the pilgrimage.

3/ Quantum Colors for Wisdom

In the Quantum Field, the colors for Wisdom for Energy Number 1 are **royal blue**, **cobalt blue**, and **aqua blue**. By placing these colors in the North area of your home and office, you are sending a strong signal to the Universe to activate your Wisdom.

4/ Wisdom Practices

You receive knowledge and wisdom most effectively by:

- Planning ahead and stating your goals
- Spending time in a monastery or on a retreat
- Spending time alone daily in meditation

- Creating a vision board of what you wish to accomplish in your life
- Walking a labyrinth, going to a powerful place, or on a pilgrimage
- Working alone
- Divining the future with astrology and oracles
- Going a vision quest
- Following your inner dreams and insights

5/ Feng Shui Activations For Your Wisdom in Your Home and Office

1. Facing Direction

When seeking knowledge or spiritual awareness, sit facing your Wisdom direction (North). It's from the North that your strongest Wisdom energy flows. You will attract greater wisdom and knowledge if you face the North whilst you're studying, at your desk, meditating, or praying.

2. Activate Your Personal Wisdom Direction: North

To attract great Wisdom, you need to activate the North areas in three places:

- Stimulate your professional wisdom by placing Feng Shui activations in the North area of your office
- Stimulate your social Wisdom by placing Feng Shui activations in the North of your living or

family room
- Stimulate your nightly insights by placing Feng Shui activations in the North of your bedroom

You can use a compass to find the correct direction. North is between 337.5 and 22.5 degrees on a compass. Make sure you are standing facing the foot end of the bed or couch, or sitting down at your desk when you hold the compass. Similarly, you can use the Diamond Compass on the Marie Diamond app that is connected with your Personal Energy Number.

Next, examine the North area of your office, living room, or bedroom. Do the items, furniture, paintings, and colors represent what you wrote down for your Wisdom goals?

For example, an image of a blocked road shows the Universe that you aren't open to new insights, so it mightn't be the best message to send to the Universe. Make sure there aren't any garbage cans or clutter in the North area because they can block the flow of energy and symbolically put your Wisdom "straight into the garbage".

Use objects that you already have in your home to activate your Wisdom area. Listed below are several options that will bring good chi to your Wisdom energy:

- Irregular or asymmetric objects
- Glass or transparent objects

- A fountain or an aquarium
- Images with a river or a waterfall or a spring
- Blue or black items
- An image of a road
- An image of a white sailboat

You can also make the space more personal by placing any of the following in your Wisdom direction:

- In your living room, an image of your church or spiritual community.
- In your office, quotes from enlightened businessmen or books on business ethics
- In your bedroom, a bible or any meditation tools

Your Vision Board

When you make a vision board, it helps to think of it as a map. The difference is that at the top of your board always represents the South and the bottom always represents the North. In order to make a vision board that creates the best results with the Law of Attraction, place a photo of you in the center and fill the vision board with the following outline:

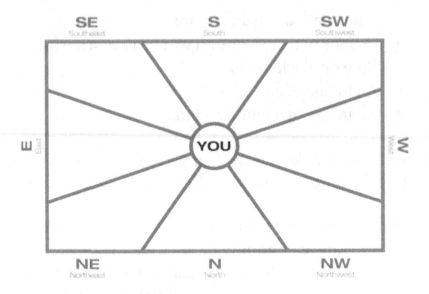

Your Success Direction

In the upper left corner: Southeast
- Write down your Success goals
- Activate it with Success images
- Activate it with the color royal blue and your quantum colors for Success

Your Health Direction

In the middle left area: East
- Write down your Health goals
- Activate it with Health images
- Activate it with the color emerald green and your quantum colors for Health

Your Relationship Direction

In the upper middle area: South
- Write down your Relationship goals
- Activate it with Relationship images
- Activate it with the color rose and your quantum colors for relationships

Your Wisdom Direction

In the center on the bottom: North
- Write down your Wisdom goals
- Activate it with Wisdom images
- Activate it with the color yellow and your quantum colors for Wisdom

The Rest of Your Vision Board

You can fill up the rest of your vision board with images that relate to more general areas of Feng Shui, such as:

- Southwest: Romance, female energy, motherhood, and collaboration
- West: Creativity, children, technology, and communication
- Northwest: Travel, advisors, friends, and space
- Northeast: Wisdom, spirituality, knowledge, and teachers
- Center: Harmony and balance

Every year, the background colors for the Vision Board change in accordance with the Yearly Law of Attraction based on Diamond Time Feng Shui.

Look for the most current Diamond Vision Board Poster, and for other Marie Diamond Feng Shui products at: http://mariediamond.com

CHAPTER 2
Energy Number 2/ 5 (Man):
The Teacher

The Information for Energy Number 2 is the Same as Energy Number 5 (Man)

Introduction

The Energy Archetype connected with Energy Number 2/ 5 (Man) is called the **Teacher**. The essence of the Teacher is:

"Wisdom sharing is your ultimate goal in life, and to do so, you will explore all possibilities to gain the right knowledge and wisdom. You like to enhance your ideas with your creativity. When people around you have problems, you are the first to offer your advice and wisdom. In addition to your words, you also offer your help. The females in your network and family will bring you great support and they are your teachers and mentors."

Famous People With This Energy Number:

Dalai Lama, Snoop Dogg, Blake Lively, and Bella Hadid

Your Best Direction for <u>Success</u> is <u>Northeast</u>

1/ Soul Journey of Success

The Energy Number 2/ 5 (Man) will be focused on having all the information they need before they move forward in their professional life. When you know the knowledge that you need, the teacher in you will step up and share it with others, as your soul is here to share knowledge and wisdom.

You will create great success in your business by studying success principles and by learning how successful people manage their companies.

Open yourself to be coached or taught by teachers of success. Don't let stress take over your professional career; find joy and peace in your daily work.

2/ Goals for Success

Affirmations share with the Universe your intention for what it is you want to accomplish in your life. But it's not just a message. There's strength in writing these goals in the present tense; you're not demanding or requesting. You're simply telling the Universe what will be. You should never write your affirmations in the future tense as there is great power in stating "This is the way I want my life to be, here and now".

Write down your Success goals on index cards, or place them on your vision board. You can also place them in the Northeast area of your living room, your bedroom, and your office.

Each goal sends your wishes to the Universe, and according to the Law of Attraction, you can attract anything you wish for. Just state your intentions and open yourself up to receive; let the Universe take care of the rest.

If you feel you don't want to place your goals out in the open, you can place them in nice, colored envelopes and address the front to the Universe, God, the Angels, or whomever you are praying to. Remember, Feng Shui is not connected with any specific religion. Instead, it respects all religions and belief systems.

Make your personal Success goals even more powerful by adding:

- An image that represents your goal
- An image of someone (such as a celebrity or someone you know personally) who has already attained a similar goal
- Any symbol that represents your goal

For Example:

You wish to become successful as a teacher or an author. Add images of famous authors, bestselling book covers, and teachers who have already accomplished this goal. Add an image of the New York Times Best Seller list logo.

3/ Quantum Colors for Success

In the Quantum Field, the colors for success for the Energy Number 2/ 5 (Man) are **yellow, saffron yellow**, and **magenta**. By placing these colors in the Northeast area of your home and office, you are sending a strong signal to the Universe to activate your success.

These colors were revealed to me after years of meditation and contemplation, and they are unique to Diamond Feng Shui.

4/ Professional Choices

For you, success and wealth are more likely when you choose the following activities or professional fields:

- Teacher, spiritual healer, or consultant
- Professor in science, biologist or librarian
- Philosopher, author, or bookseller
- Mountain climber
- Learning disabilities specialist
- Publisher or tour guide
- Journalist or minister
- Database manager

5/ Feng Shui Activations For Your Success in Your Home and Office

1. Facing Direction

During the day, make sure you're facing your Success direction (Northeast) whilst working or meeting up with clients. It's from the Northeast that your strongest Success energy flows. Your ability to attract Success increases greatly when you face towards the Northeast whilst you're working, sitting at your desk, looking at your computer screen, when meeting with people, negotiating, and signing contracts.

Avoid sitting with your back to the door since it's poor Feng Shui. From an evolutionary standpoint, our early ancestors faced a lot of dangers in their lives. From wild animals to attacks from other tribes, they had to be completely aware of their surroundings in order to survive. So, from that viewpoint, it makes sense to have a clear view of your door when you're sitting down or in bed so that you know exactly who's coming into the room. If you can't see the door, you make yourself vulnerable to people sneaking up on you. In terms of Feng Shui, you want to make sure you're in the path of the incoming flow of positive energy. You want to see all the good opportunities that enter through the door, and you want to make sure you're making yourself accessible to any good fortune that comes knocking.

2. Activate your Success Direction: Northeast

To attract great Success, you need to activate the Northeast area in three places.

- Professional success is focused in the Northeast area of your office
- Personal success is focused in the Northeast area of your living room or family room
- Romantic success is focused in the Northeast of your bedroom

You can use a compass to find the correct direction. Northeast is between 22.5 and 67.5 degrees on a compass. Make sure you are standing facing the foot end of the bed or couch, or sitting down at your desk when you hold the compass. Similarly, you can use the Diamond Compass on the Marie Diamond app that is connected with your Personal Energy Number.

Next, examine the Northeast area of your office, living room, and bedroom. Do the items, furniture, paintings, and colors represent what you wrote down for your Success goals?

For example, if you have a painting of a sinking ship, is this representative of an exceptional career? Make sure there aren't any garbage cans or clutter in the Northeast area because they can block the flow of energy and symbolically put your Success "straight into the garbage".

Use objects that you already have in your home to activate your Success area. Listed below are several options that will bring good chi to your Success energy:

- Square or cubical objects
- Ceramic or crystal objects
- Images and statues of praying or meditating saints and masters
- Beige, orange, yellow, turquoise, red, rose, or purple objects
- Books on success or on your professional focus

- Your awards and certificates
- Image of a mountain (but not one that's completely covered in snow)
- Lotus flowers
- Candles
- Amethyst gemstones

In the office, you can also make the space more personal by placing any of the following in your Success direction:

- The logo of your company
- Your products or designs
- Your vision board with your goals
- A personal success affirmation card
- Books written by your coaches, mentors, and teachers
- Certificates of your studies and trainings

Your Best Direction for <u>Health</u> is <u>West</u>

1/ Soul Journey of Health

Energy Number 2/ 5 (Man) needs to be able to express their deepest fears and pain. Release work is essential. They are typically people that have deep, dark secrets, as deep as lakes. They may feel unwilling to burden others with their pain, but this can lead to them trying to cope with everything by themselves. This can create a negative force field within themselves that can sometimes become a physical pain.

Creating better health is more likely to happen when you deal with your emotional traumas from your childhood. Do some laughter therapy and take steps to make your everyday life more enjoyable. Relax at the beach, enjoy surfing and sailing.

Make sure you take care of your teeth as this can affect your whole immune system. Smile and you will feel better.

2/ Goals for Health

Write down your Health goals on index cards, or place them on your vision board. You can also place them in the West area of your living room, your bedroom, and your office.

Each goal sends your wishes to the Universe, and according to the Law of Attraction, you can attract anything you wish for. Just state your intentions and open yourself up to receive; let the Universe take care of the rest.

If you feel you don't want to place your goals out in the open, you can place them in nice, colored envelopes and address the front to the Universe, God, the Angels, or whomever you are praying to. Remember, Feng Shui is not connected with any specific religion. Instead, it respects all religions and belief systems.

Make your personal Health goals even more powerful by adding:

- An image that represents your goal
- An image of someone (such as a celebrity or someone you know personally) who has already attained a similar goal
- Any symbol that represents your goal

For Example:

You wish to have beautiful teeth. Add images of someone who you think has the perfect smile. Add the business card of the best dentist in town.

3/ Quantum Colors for Health

In the Quantum Field, the colors for Health for the Energy Number 2/5 (Male) are **white**, **ivory white**, and **peach**. By placing these colors in the West areas of your home and office, you are sending a strong signal to the Universe to activate your Health.

4/ Health Practices

The following suggestions can help enhance your health energy. These suggestions will not guarantee your health, but instead will make it easier for you to become healthier.

- Focus on being playful and joyful in your life
- Play with your children or grandchildren

- Be creative, dance, and sing
- Snorkel or swim with dolphins
- Allow your children take care of you when you're sick
- Take care of your teeth to improve your general health
- Energize yourself at the beach

5/ Feng Shui Activations For Your Health in Your Home and Office

1. Facing Direction

When you're in bed, sleep with the top of your head pointing toward your Health direction (West). During the day, sit in your living space or in your dining room facing your health direction.

Your energy level will increase when you sleep with the crown of your head pointing toward this direction, so arrange your bed so you can do so. If you lie on your couch when you're ill, make sure the top of your head faces the West.

2. Activate Your personal Health Direction: West

To attract good Health, you need to activate the West in three places:

- To stimulate your energy for health when you're working, place Feng Shui activations in

the West area of your office. A healthy worker creates a healthy business
- Place Feng Shui activations in the West of your living or family room so that during the daytime, you're creating good energy
- Place Feng Shui activations in the West of your bedroom to stimulate your health whilst you're sleeping and to help you wake up energized in the morning

You can use a compass to find the correct direction. West is between 247.5 and 292.5 degrees on a compass. Make sure you are standing facing the foot end of the bed or couch, or sitting down at your desk when you hold the compass. Similarly, you can use the Diamond Compass on the Marie Diamond app that is connected with your Personal Energy Number.

Next, examine the West corner of your office, living room, or bedroom. Do the items, furniture, paintings, and colors represent what you wrote down for your Health goals?

For example, if you have an image from the Star Wars movie in your Health area, don't be surprised if you find yourself fighting the Dark Side (illness)! Make sure there aren't any garbage cans or clutter in the West area because they can block the flow of energy and symbolically put your health "straight into the garbage".

Use objects that you already have in your home to activate your Health direction. Listed below are several objects that will bring good chi to your Health energy:

- Round or oval objects
- Metal objects
- Artwork or crafts
- Playful objects, toys, and gadgets
- White, silver or gold objects
- Ceramic or crystal objects
- Pictures of children playing
- An image with white boats sailing on a lake or ocean
- Objects connected with the wind, such as flags or windsocks
- Metal wind chimes (either 6 or 7 hollow metal tubes are best)
- Gemstones

You can also make the space more personal by placing any of the following in your Health direction:

- An image of yourself when you appeared radiant and healthy in your living room
- Your vitamins, food supplements, workout or exercise equipment in your bedroom
- Books on health, yoga or relaxation in your office

Your Best Direction for <u>Relationships</u> is <u>Northwest</u>

1/ Soul Journey of Relationships

Energy Number 2/5 (Man) will most likely attract people from other countries and cultures, or maybe even a younger partner. They will enjoy traveling together during their relationships. This soul is learning not to have prejudices or judgments towards other people from different races.

You are looking for a romantic partner who will also be a great supporter, coach, and mentor in your life. You will feel as if your partner is heaven-sent. You love taking your family on trips to other countries, or at least enjoy eating foreign foods with them in your own city. Your business can attract international clients.

2/ Goals for Relationships

Write down your Relationship goals on index cards, or place them on your vision board. You can also place them in the Northwest area of your living room, your bedroom, and your office.

Each goal sends your wishes to the Universe, and according to the Law of Attraction, you can attract anything you wish for. Just state your intentions and open yourself up to receive; let the Universe take care of the rest.

If you feel you don't want to place your goals out in the open, you can place them in nice, colored envelopes and address the front to the Universe, God, the Angels, or whomever you are praying to. Remember, Feng Shui is not connected with any specific religion. Instead, it respects all religions and belief systems.

Make your personal Relationship goals even more powerful by adding:

- An image that represents your goal
- An image of someone (such as a celebrity or someone you know personally) who has already attained a similar goal
- Any symbol that represents your goal

For Example:

You wish to go on a holiday cruise to Greece with your family. Add images of a family on a cruise boat, pages from a travel brochure, and images of Greek temples and islands.

Special Tip

Single women who want to have a steady romantic relationship should place peonies in their personal relationship direction. They can be real, silk, or just an image. Once you have attracted the relationship you wished for, give the peonies to someone who wishes to have the same kind of luck. Don't keep them. Men can do the same thing but use a bamboo plant instead of peonies.

3/ Quantum Colors for Relationships

In the Quantum Field, the colors for Relationships for Energy Number 2/5 (Man) are **opal**, **diamond**, and **silver**. By placing these colors in the Northwest area of your home and office, you are sending a strong signal to the Universe to activate your Relationships.

4/ Relationship Practices

The following are characteristic of those with an Energy Number of 2/ 5 (Man):

- Your purpose for relationships is to focus on advising your partners and to let God or the Universe to support you. Pray for your relationships
- You will protect your loved ones with the power of Angels
- You are open for coaching or counseling sessions to improve your relationships
- You attract partners or friends from other countries or cultures
- Women can attract partners that they view as father-figures
- Men can attract partners that are younger
- You will enjoy gazing at the stars and the planets together

- You may meet your partner at a spiritual event
- You teach your children other languages
- The colors that stimulate your relationships are white, silver, gold, and earth tones like yellow, beige, and orange
- You connect with the power of metal and gemstones
- You may adopt a child from another country
- You may like to join the Peace Corps or do volunteer work with other cultures
- You love traveling with your family

5/ Feng Shui Activations For Your Relationships in your Home and Office

1. Facing Direction

Make sure you sit facing, or sleep with your head pointing towards your Relationship direction (Northwest) in order to attract good relationships.

During the day, face the Northwest when you're in the office, attending business meetings, dinners, or important conferences and you will be much more successful with your business relationships.

2. Activate Your Personal Relationship Direction: Northwest

To attract better relationships, activate the Northwest in three places:

- For excellent professional relationships, focus on the Northwest area of your office
- For family relationships, focus on the Northwest area of your family or living room
- To stimulate your personal relationship, focus on the Northwest area of your bedroom

You can use a compass to find the correct direction. Northwest is between 292.5 and 337.5 degrees on a compass. Make sure you are standing facing the foot end of the bed or couch, or sitting down at your desk when you hold the compass. Similarly, you can use the Diamond Compass on the Marie Diamond app that is connected with your Personal Energy Number.

Next, examine the Northwest area of your office, living room, or bedroom. Do the items, furniture, paintings, and colors represent what you wrote down for your Relationship goals?

For example, if you have an image of a couple dancing in the rain, the rain symbolizes emotional struggles between the two people and that the relationship will not last. Make sure there aren't any garbage cans or clutter in the Northwest area because they can block the flow of energy and symbolically put your relationships "straight into the garbage".

Use objects that you already have in your home to activate your relationship direction.

Listed below are several options that will bring good chi to your Relationship energy:

- Round or oval objects
- Metal objects
- White, silver, or gold object
- Ceramic or crystal objects
- Images of you with your father or of you with your children
- Images of space, the moon, stars, and planets
- Metal wind chimes (one with 6 rods and hollow metal tubes is best)
- Gemstones
- Images of your mentor or coach
- Images of presidents, old wise men, spiritual teachers, or religious leaders
- Objects that make you feel closer to heaven and God
- Images of Angels or fairies

You can also make the space more personal by placing any of the following in your Relationship direction:

- In your office, display a photo of your professional team, or of you and your manager. Also, place your address book or business cards from your clients in the Northwest area
- In your living or family room, display recent photos of you with your loved ones. Also, photos of you and your friends
- In your bedroom, place photos of you with your

romantic partner

Your Best Direction for <u>Wisdom</u> is <u>Southwest</u>

1/ Soul Journey of Wisdom

You will feel stimulated by the wisdom and knowledge of women. When you look back on your life, you'll realize that you received the best advice from women. Or, perhaps you were devoted and prayed to a female saint or followed your spiritual journey with a female teacher.

You also love taking care of others. Your advice tends to be accepted more readily by women than men. Praying to and meditating toward divine mothers will nurture you. Your mother, grandmother, or big sister will be a source of wisdom and knowledge for you.
You'll learn that most of your spiritual lessons will come from being married or romantically involved. Your business partners will also inspire you.

2/ Goals for Wisdom

Write down your Wisdom goals on index cards, or place them on your vision board. You can also place them in the Southwest area of your living room, your bedroom, and your office.

Each goal sends your wishes to the Universe, and according to the Law of Attraction, you can attract anything you wish for. Just state your intentions and open yourself up to receive; let the Universe take care of the rest.

If you feel you don't want to place your goals out in the open, you can place them in nice, colored envelopes and address the front to the Universe, God, the Angels, or whomever you are praying to. Remember, Feng Shui is not connected with any specific religion. Instead, it respects all religions and belief systems.

Make your personal Wisdom goals even more powerful by adding:

- An image that represents your goal
- An image of someone (such as a celebrity or someone you know personally) who has already attained a similar goal
- Any symbol that represents your goal

For Example:

You wish to have spiritual practice with a romantic partner. Add images of a couple meditating together. You can also add an image of two lotus flowers in a pond.

3/ Quantum Colors for Wisdom

In the Quantum Field, the colors for Wisdom for Energy Number 2/ 5 (Man) are **rose**, **pink**, and **fuchsia**. By placing these colors in the Southwest area of your home and office, you are sending a strong signal to the Universe to activate your Wisdom.

4/ Wisdom Practices

You receive knowledge and wisdom most effectively by:

- Connecting with the wisdom of native communities
- Opening yourself to the wisdom of the earth
- Dowsing and knowing how the magnetic field of the earth works with you
- Learning how to cook and knowing about healthy food
- Talking to your female ancestors
- Collaborating more with women in your job
- Going to relationship therapy
- Learning about the spiritual side of sexuality
- Connecting with divine mothers
- Surrounding yourself with gemstones
- Meditating or praying together with your romantic partner and your family

5/ Feng Shui Activations For Your Wisdom in Your Home and Office

1. Facing Direction

When seeking knowledge or spiritual awareness, sit facing your Wisdom direction (Southwest). It's from the Southwest that your strongest Wisdom energy flows. You will attract greater wisdom and knowledge if you face the Southwest whilst you're studying, at your desk, meditating, or praying.

2. Activate Your Personal Wisdom Direction: Southwest

To attract great Wisdom, you need to activate the Southwest areas in three places:

- Stimulate your professional wisdom by placing Feng Shui activations in the Southwest area of your office
- Stimulate your social Wisdom by placing Feng Shui activations in the Southwest of your living or family room
- Stimulate your nightly insights by placing Feng Shui activations in the Southwest of your bedroom

You can use a compass to find the correct direction. Southwest is between 202.5 and 247.5 degrees on a compass. Make sure you are standing facing the foot end of the bed or couch, or sitting down at your desk when you hold the compass. Similarly, you can use the Diamond Compass on the Marie Diamond app that is connected with your Personal Energy Number.

Next, examine the Southwest area of your office, living room, or bedroom. Do the items, furniture, paintings, and colors represent what you wrote down for your

Wisdom goals?

For example, having an image here of a veiled woman shows that you are not open to information. Make sure there aren't any garbage cans or clutter in the Southwest area because they can block the flow of energy and symbolically put your Wisdom "straight into the garbage".

Use objects that you already have in your home to activate your Wisdom area. Listed below are several options that will bring good chi to your Wisdom energy:

- Square or cubical objects
- Ceramic or crystal objects
- A large rose quartz heart
- Spiritual or religious items, displayed in pairs
- The double happiness symbol
- A crystal globe
- An image of a compassionate mother like Lady Mary
- Two red or rose candles
- An image of a mother and baby animal

You can also make the space more personal by placing any of the following in your Wisdom direction:

- In your living room, display an image of your church or spiritual community
- In your office, display quotes from enlightened

businessmen or books on business ethics

Your Vision Board

When you make a vision board, it helps to think of it as a map. The difference is that at the top of your board always represents the South and the bottom always represents the North. In order to make a vision board that creates the best results with the Law of Attraction, place a photo of you in the center and fill the vision board with the following outline:

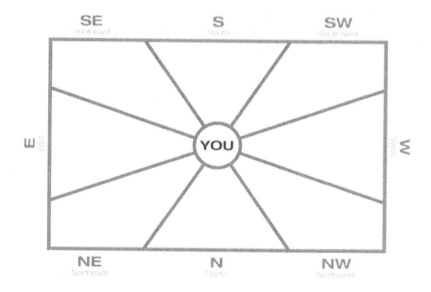

Your Success Direction

In the lower left corner: Northeast
- Write down your Success goals
- Activate it with Success images
- Activate it with the color royal blue and your

quantum colors for Success

Your Health Direction

In the middle right area: West
- Write down your Health goals
- Activate it with Health images
- Activate it with the color emerald green and your quantum colors for Health

Your Relationship Direction

In the lower right corner: Northwest
- Write down your Relationship goals
- Activate it with Relationship images
- Activate it with the color rose and your quantum colors for relationships

Your Wisdom Direction

In the upper right corner: Southwest
- Write down your Wisdom goals
- Activate it with Wisdom images
- Activate it with the color yellow and your quantum colors for Wisdom

The Rest of Your Vision Board

You can fill up the rest of your vision board with images that relate to more general areas of Feng Shui, such as:

- South: Self-esteem, entertainment, enlightenment, dance, and music
- North: Career and traveling
- East: Family, health, government, elders, and the past
- Southeast: Money, luxury, and good fortune
- Center: Harmony and balance

Every year, the background colors for the Vision Board change in accordance with the Yearly Law of Attraction based on Diamond Time Feng Shui.

Look for the most current Diamond Vision Board Poster, and for other Marie Diamond Feng Shui products at: http://mariediamond.com

CHAPTER 3
Energy Number 3:
The Bringer of Light

Introduction

The Energy Archetype connected with Energy Number 3 is called the **Bringer of Light**. The essence of the Bringer of Light is:

"By creating music and dance you bring life and light to people. Life is full of passion and change. Let go of all stress in your professional life. Friends are your treasures and will always bring you good fortune. Family life will give you inspiration and wisdom."

Famous People With This Energy Number:

Lizzo, Robin Williams, Kylie Jenner, and Adele

Your Best Direction for <u>Success</u> is <u>South</u>

1/ Soul Journey of Success

The Soul of Energy Number 3 is here to live life fully, to be visible, and to share their inner light through music and dance. Their passion is greater than anyone else's for their professional career. When there's no passion, they feel lost.

When they're not able to express themselves, they dim their light. You have an interest in music, dance, and performance. You're an artist passionate about your work and searching for recognition and fame. You can help people sparkle and shine in their lives.

2/ Goals for Success

Affirmations share with the Universe your intention for what it is you want to accomplish in your life. But it's not just a message. There's strength in writing these goals in the present tense; you're not demanding or requesting. You're simply telling the Universe what will be. You should never write your affirmations in the future tense as there is great power in stating "This is the way I want my life to be, here and now".

Write down your Success goals on index cards, or place them on your vision board. You can also place them in the South area of your living room, your bedroom, and your office.

Each goal sends your wishes to the Universe, and according to the Law of Attraction, you can attract anything you wish for. Just state your intentions and open yourself up to receive; let the Universe take care of the rest.

If you feel you don't want to place your goals out in the open, you can place them in nice, colored envelopes and address the front to the Universe, God, the Angels, or whomever you are praying to. Remember, Feng Shui is not connected with any specific religion. Instead, it respects all religions and belief systems.

Make your personal Success goals even more powerful by adding:

- An image that represents your goal
- An image of someone (such as a celebrity or someone you know personally) who has already attained a similar goal
- Any symbol that represents your goal

For Example:

You want to become a very famous and successful actress. Add images of someone who is very famous and respected as an actress. Add images of awards with your name on them such as an Oscar statue for Best Actress.

3/ Quantum Colors for Success

In the Quantum Field, the colors for Success for the Energy Number 3 are **ruby red**, **cherry red**, and **orange**. By placing these colors in the South area of your home and office, you are sending a strong signal to the Universe to activate your Success.

These colors were revealed to me after years of meditation and contemplation, and they are unique to Diamond Feng Shui.

4/ Professional Choices

For you, success and wealth are more likely when you choose the following activities or professional fields:

- Dancer, film producer, or actor or actress
- Worker in the theater or opera
- Lighting or candle specialist
- Self-esteem coach
- Musician or musical director
- An agent for artists
- Fashion designer, colorist, or painter
- Singer and spiritual teacher

5/ Feng Shui Activations For Your Success in Your Home and Office

1. Facing Direction

During the day, make sure you're facing your Success direction (South) whilst working or meeting up with clients. It's from the South that your strongest Success energy flows. Your ability to attract Success increases greatly when you face towards the South whilst you're working, sitting at your desk, looking at your computer screen, when meeting with people, negotiating, and signing contracts.

Avoid sitting with your back to the door since it's poor Feng Shui. From an evolutionary standpoint, our early ancestors faced a lot of dangers in their lives.

From wild animals to attacks from other tribes, they had to be completely aware of their surroundings in order to survive. So, from that viewpoint, it makes sense to have a clear view of your door when you're sitting down or in bed so that you know exactly who's coming into the room. If you can't see the door, you make yourself vulnerable to people sneaking up on you.

In terms of Feng Shui, you want to make sure you're in the path of the incoming flow of positive energy. You want to see all the good opportunities that enter through the door, and you want to make sure you're making yourself accessible to any good fortune that comes knocking.

2. Activate Your Personal Success Direction: South

To attract great Success, you need to activate the South area in three places:

- Professional success is focused in the South area of your office.
- Personal success is focused in the South area of your living room or family room.
- Romantic and family success is focused in the South area of your bedroom.

You can use a compass to find the correct direction. South is between 157.5 and 202.5 degrees on a compass. Make sure you are standing facing the foot end of the bed or couch, or sitting down at your desk when you hold the compass. Similarly, you can use the Diamond Compass on the Marie Diamond app that is connected with your Personal Energy Number.

Next, examine the South area of your office, living room, or bedroom. Do the items, furniture, paintings, and colors represent what you wrote down for your Success goals?

For example, an image of someone sitting down with his head in his hands does not look like someone with passion in his life. Make sure there aren't any garbage cans or clutter in the South area because they can block the flow of energy and symbolically put your Success "straight into the garbage".

Use objects that you already have in your home to activate your Success area. Listed below are several options that will bring good chi to your Success energy:

- Triangle or pyramid-shaped objects, stripy objects, and long and tall objects
- Objects made of plastic or wood
- Images of flowers and plants (but no plants with spiky leaves such as cactus, palm trees, or yuccas as they create attacking energy in your living space)
- Real flowers and plants (again, no spiky leaves because they pick away at your success. Also make sure the plants are not as high as trees)
- Silk flowers and plastic plants (but not dried

flowers or plants)
- Fire colors such as red, purple, yellow, orange, rose, fuchsia, brown, beige, and green-colored objects
- Magazines and books about show business, art, music, and performance
- Candles
- Images of famous musicians, dancers, and singers

In your office, you can also make the space more personal by placing any of the following in your Success direction:

- The logo of your company
- Your products or designs
- Your vision board with your goals
- A personal success affirmation card

Your Best Direction for Health is North

1/ Soul Journey for Health

Energy Number 3 would still show up to work or perform in a dance recital even if they are in the greatest of pain. This pride can create problems for them.

After a crisis, know that you're not alone and that you need to relax and let others take care of things. Carrying everything alone on your shoulders creates too much stress on yourself.

You can stay fit and healthy by swimming, scuba diving, or sailing. Taking showers or long relaxing baths will help you let go of the stress of your job. Focus on maintaining a healthy body and working out. Don't worry about your health when you're retired. You may have issues with water retention.

2/ Goals for Health

Write down your Health goals on index cards, or place them on your vision board. You can also place them in the North area of your living room, your bedroom, and your office.

Each goal sends your wishes to the Universe, and according to the Law of Attraction, you can attract anything you wish for. Just state your intentions and open yourself up to receive; let the Universe take care of the rest.

If you feel you don't want to place your goals out in the open, you can place them in nice, colored envelopes and address the front to the Universe, God, the Angels, or whomever you are praying to. Remember, Feng Shui is not connected with any specific religion. Instead, it respects all religions and belief systems.

Make your personal Health goals even more powerful by adding:

- An image that represents your goal
- An image of someone (such as a celebrity or someone you know personally) who has already attained a similar goal
- Any symbol that represents your goal

For Example:

You want to lose weight. Add images of someone who has lost a substantial amount of weight such as Oprah Winfrey. You can add the clothing size that you wish to fight into.

3/ Quantum Colors for Health

In the Quantum Field, the colors for Health for the Energy Number 3 are **royal blue**, **cobalt blue**, and **aqua blue**. By placing these colors in the North, you are sending a strong signal to the Universe to activate your Health.

4/ Health Practices

The following suggestions can help enhance your health energy. These suggestions will not guarantee your health, but instead will make it easier for you to become healthier:

- Focus on being relaxed about your future and try to go with the flow. Maintain a positive attitude for what lies ahead
- Always take special care of your ears, especially from harsh noises or loud music. Also remember that not everything you hear is the truth, so check it out first before you get upset
- Your work has a great influence on your health, especially your relationship with your boss. Relax more and just do your best. The more stress you create about holding on to your job, the more you will feel drained of energy. There is more to life than your job, even if you are passionate about it
- Try to find a better balance between your career and your home life
- Take care of your heart by eating healthy foods.
- Drink more water and don't eat too much salt.
- Take it easy with alcohol, especially clear liquors
- Make sure you shower every day before or after work, or take a long bath with essential oils to relax
- On the weekends go sailing, scuba diving or canoeing, or take walks alone along the water to bring good health to your body
- Swim with dolphins
- Go fishing or spend time sitting by a creek
- Don't try to be healthy alone – ask your family and friends to help you.

5/ Feng Shui Activation For Your Health in Your Home and Office

1. Facing Direction

When you're in bed, sleep with the top of your head pointing toward your Health direction (North). During the day, sit in your living space or in your dining room facing your health direction.

Your energy level will increase when you sleep with the crown of your head pointing toward this direction, so arrange your bed so you can do so. If you lie on your couch when you're ill, make sure the top of your head faces the North.

2. Activate Your Personal Health Direction: North

To attract good Health, you need to activate the North in three places:

- To stimulate your energy for health when you're working, place Feng Shui activations in the North area of your office. A healthy worker creates a healthy business
- Place Feng Shui activations in the North of your living or family room so that during the daytime, you're creating good energy
- Place Feng Shui activations in the North of your bedroom to stimulate your health whilst you're sleeping and to help you wake up energized in the morning

You can use a compass to find the correct direction. North is between 337.5 and 22.5 degrees on a compass. Make sure you are standing facing the foot end of the bed or couch, or sitting down at your desk when you hold the compass. Similarly, you can use the Diamond Compass on the Marie Diamond app that is connected with your Personal Energy Number.

Next, examine the North corner of your office, living room, or bedroom. Do the items, furniture, paintings, and colors represent what you wrote down for your Health goals?

For example, an image of a swamp can create poor immunity. Make sure there aren't any garbage cans or clutter in the North area because they can block the flow of energy and symbolically put your Health "straight into the garbage".

Use objects that you already have in your home to activate your health direction. Listed below are several options that will bring good chi to your Health energy:

- Irregular or asymmetric objects
- Glass or transparent objects
- A fountain or an aquarium
- Images of a river or a waterfall
- Blue or black items
- An image of a road
- An image of a white sailboat

You can also make the space more personal by placing any of the following in your Health direction:

- An image of yourself when you appeared radiant and healthy in your living room
- Your vitamins, food supplements, workout or exercise equipment in your bedroom
- Books on health, yoga or relaxation in your office

Your Best Direction for <u>Relationships </u>is <u>Southeast</u>

1/ Soul Journey of Relationships

The soul of an Energy Number 3 sees their relationships as their greatest assets. Once they find their true love, they cherish it but it can take a long time for them to find that special someone.

Having a great relationship with someone is something you see as a great fortune in your life. People are like treasures to you. Friends are jewels in your life.

You would like to spend time with your loved ones sailing on a yacht. You love spending money for the ones you love. You would give your last dime away in order to make your relationships work.

2/ Goals for Relationships

Write down your Relationship goals on index cards, or place them on your vision board. You can also place them in the Southeast area of your living room, your bedroom, and your office.

Each goal sends your wishes to the Universe, and according to the Law of Attraction, you can attract anything you wish for. Just state your intentions and open yourself up to receive; let the Universe take care of the rest.

If you feel you don't want to place your goals out in the open, you can place them in nice, colored envelopes and address the front to the Universe, God, the Angels, or whomever you are praying to. Remember, Feng Shui is not connected with any specific religion. Instead, it respects all religions and belief systems.

Make your personal Relationship goals even more powerful by adding:

- An image that represents your goal
- An image of someone (such as a celebrity or someone you know personally) who has already attained a similar goal
- Any symbol that represents your goal

For Example:

You want to attract wealthy friends. Add images of a group of people living a luxury lifestyle. You can add images of yachts, luxury cars, and money.

Special Tip

Single women who want to have a steady romantic relationship should place peonies in their personal relationship direction. They can be real, silk, or just an image. Once you have attracted the relationship you wished for, give the peonies to someone who wishes to have the same kind of luck. Don't keep them. Men can do the same thing but use a bamboo plant instead of peonies.

3/ Quantum Colors for Relationships

In the Quantum Field, the colors for Relationships for the Energy Number 3 are **violet**, **lilac**, and **gold**. By placing these colors in the Southeast area of your home and office, you are sending a strong signal to the Universe to activate your Relationships.

4/ Relationship Practices

The following are characteristic of those with an Energy Number of 3:

- You focus on bringing good luck to your loved ones

- You view finding good friends like treasure hunting. Once you've found them, you don't let go and you appreciate them forever
- You will attract a loving partner who is financially independent or is someone who brings large amounts of money into your relationship
- You would like to be business partners with your romantic partner
- The colors that stimulate your relationships are green, brown, lilac, and purple
- You connect with the power of plants and flowers. You regularly give your partners and friends bouquets of their favorite flowers
- You bless your life daily and appreciate your good fortune
- You like to picnic in the grass with your romantic partner
- You enjoy being with your partner near water, either by a river, at a waterfall, or just by taking a shower together

5/ Feng Shui Activations For Your Relationships in Your Home and Office

1. Facing Direction

Make sure you sit facing, or sleep with your head pointing towards your Relationship direction (Southeast) in order to attract good relationships.

During the day, face the Southeast when you're in the office, attending business meetings, dinners, or important conferences and you will be much more successful with your business relationships.

2. Activate Your Relationship Direction: Southeast

To attract better relationships, activate the Southeast in three places:

- For excellent professional relationships, focus on the Southeast area of your office
- For family relationships, focus on the Southeast area of your family or living room
- To stimulate your personal relationship, focus on the Southeast area of your bedroom

You can use a compass to find the correct direction. Southeast is between 112.5 and 157.5 degrees on a compass. Make sure you are standing facing the foot end of the bed or couch, or sitting down at your desk when you hold the compass. Similarly, you can use the Diamond Compass on the Marie Diamond app that is connected with your Personal Energy Number.

Next, examine the Southeast area of your office, living room, or bedroom. Do the items, furniture, paintings, and colors represent what you wrote down for your Relationship goals?

For example, if you have an image of a single flower, do not be surprised if you don't attract a partner in your life. Make sure there aren't any garbage cans or clutter in the Southeast area because they can block the flow of energy and symbolically put romance and passion "straight into the garbage".

Use objects that you already have in your home to activate your relationship direction. Listed below are several options that will bring good chi to your Relationship energy:

- Cylinder-shaped objects, objects with stripes, or long and tall objects
- Objects made of wood
- Images of flowers and plants (your plants should not have spiky leaves such as cactus, palm trees, or yuccas because they create attacking energy in your living space)
- Real flowers and plants (Again, don't use plants with spiky leaves because they pick away at your success)
- Silk flowers and plastic plants (but not dried flowers or plants)
- Brown, beige, green, and lilac-colored objects
- Magazines and books on financial advice or creating wealth and money
- A wealth ship, a money frog, or a bowl with coins
- Images and books about millionaires and billionaires
- Items arranged together in groups of four (such as four bamboo sticks)

- A small fountain
- An image of a small waterfall or of a river in a green lush landscape

You can also make the space more personal by placing any of the following in your Relationship direction:

- In your office, display a photo of your professional team, or of you and your manager. Also, place your address book or business cards from your clients in the South area
- In your living or family room, display recent photos of you with your loved ones. Also, photos of you and your friends
- In your bedroom, place photos of you with your romantic partner. Photos of you with your children can work here too, but not of you with your mother-in-law

Your Best Direction for <u>Wisdom</u> is <u>East</u>

1/ Soul Journey of Wisdom

A Soul with Energy Number 3 has a hard time listening to others. They may feel like they know best all the time. It's humbleness that is their major lesson to learn. They may learn it the hard way, as they aren't always ready to listen to the elders in their family or even to their teachers. They could have an easier spiritual life if their ego would be more willing to listen to good advice. It's important to listen to the wisdom of the elders in your own family and from your community.

Releasing the past and learning to forgive yourself will also help you to grow spiritually. Connecting with nature and working with plants, trees, and herbs will inspire you.

2/ Goals for Wisdom

Write down your Wisdom goals on index cards, or place them on your vision board. You can also place them in the East area of your living room, your bedroom, and your office.

Each goal sends your wishes to the Universe, and according to the Law of Attraction, you can attract anything you wish for. Just state your intentions and open yourself up to receive; let the Universe take care of the rest.

If you feel you don't want to place your goals out in the open, you can place them in nice, colored envelopes and address the front to the Universe, God, the Angels, or whomever you are praying to. Remember, Feng Shui is not connected with any specific religion. Instead, it respects all religions and belief systems.

Make your personal Wisdom goals even more powerful by adding:

- An image that represents your goal

- An image of someone (such as a celebrity or someone you know personally) who has already attained a similar goal
- Any symbol that represents your goal

For Example:

You want to connect more with nature. Add images of places in nature that inspire you. You can add images of beautiful landscapes.

3/ Quantum Colors for Wisdom

In the Quantum Field, the colors for Wisdom for the Energy Number 3 are **emerald green, citrus green** and **iris blue**. By placing these colors in the east area of your home and office, you are sending a strong signal to the Universe to activate your Wisdom.

4/ Wisdom Practices

You receive knowledge and wisdom most effectively by:

- Connecting with your own past
- Creating your family tree to learn about your ancestors
- Releasing your traumas and starting fresh with a clean slate
- Studying history
- Listening to the ancient wisdom keepers

- Walking barefoot in the grass in the morning to increase your intuition
- Shopping for antiques will inspire you
- Studying trees, flowers, and plants to allow you time for reflection

5/ Feng Shui Activations For Your Wisdom in Your Home and Office

1. Facing Direction

When seeking knowledge or spiritual awareness, sit facing your Wisdom direction (East). It's from the East that your strongest Wisdom energy flows. You will attract greater wisdom and knowledge if you face the East whilst you're studying, at your desk, meditating, or praying.

2. Activate Your Personal Wisdom Direction: East

To attract great Wisdom, you need to activate the East areas in three places:

- Stimulate your professional wisdom by placing Feng Shui activations in the East area of your office
- Stimulate your social Wisdom by placing Feng Shui activations in the East of your living or family room
- Stimulate your nightly insights by placing Feng Shui activations in the East of your bedroom

You can use a compass to find the correct direction. East is between 67.5 and 112.5 degrees on a compass. Make sure you are standing facing the foot end of the bed or couch, or sitting down at your desk when you hold the compass. Similarly, you can use the Diamond Compass on the Marie Diamond app that is connected with your Personal Energy Number.

Next, examine the East area of your office, living room, or bedroom. Do the items, furniture, paintings, and colors represent what you wrote down for your Wisdom goals?

For example, an image of chopped-down trees shows you are not in touch with heaven. Make sure there aren't any garbage cans or clutter in the East area because they can block the flow of energy and symbolically put your Wisdom "straight into the garbage".

Use objects that you already have in your home to activate your wisdom area. Listed below are several options that will bring good chi to your Wisdom energy:

- Long and tall objects, or objects with stripes
- Wooden and glass objects
- Antiques
- Flowers and plants
- Images of flowers and plants and forest and gardens

- Brown and green objects
- Pictures of your elders
- Pictures of springtime or of a mountain spring
- Images of a river or a fountain

You can also make the space more personal by placing any of the following in your Wisdom direction:

- In your living room, an image of your church or spiritual community.
- In your office, quotes from enlightened businessmen or books on business ethics
- In your bedroom, a bible or any meditation tools

Your Vision Board

When you make a vision board, it helps to think of it as a map. The difference is that at the top of your board always represents the South and the bottom always represents the North.

In order to make a vision board that creates the best results with the Law of Attraction, place a photo of you in the center and fill the vision board with the following outline:

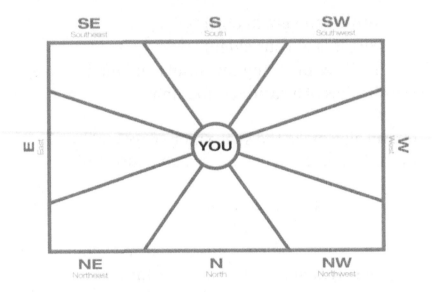

Your Success Direction

In the upper center: South
- Write down your Success goals
- Activate it with Success images
- Activate it with the color royal blue and your quantum colors for Success

Your Health Direction

In the bottom center: North
- Write down your Health goals
- Activate it with Health images
- Activate it with the color emerald green and your quantum colors for Health

Your Relationship Direction

In the upper left corner: Southeast
- Write down your Relationship goals
- Activate it with Relationship images
- Activate it with the color rose and your quantum colors for relationships

Your Wisdom Direction

In the center left: East
- Write down your Wisdom goals
- Activate it with Wisdom images
- Activate it with the color yellow and your quantum colors for Wisdom

The Rest of Your Vision Board

You can fill up the rest of your vision board with images that relate to more general areas of Feng Shui, such as:
- Southwest: Romance, female energy, motherhood, and collaboration
- West: Creativity, children, technology, and communication
- Northwest: Travel, advisors, friends, and space
- Northeast: Wisdom, spirituality, knowledge, and teachers
- Center: Harmony and balance

Every year, the background colors for the Vision Board change in accordance with the Yearly Law of Attraction based on Diamond Time Feng Shui.

Look for the most current Diamond Vision Board Poster, and for other Marie Diamond Feng Shui products at: http://mariediamond.com

CHAPTER 4
Energy Number 4:
The Manager

Introduction

The Energy Archetype connected with Energy number 4 is called the **Manager**. The essence of the Manager is:

"With a clear vision of the future you start projects, planning and organizing every step until they are finished with perfection. Nature is a resource of happiness for your relationships with family and friends. You enjoy the sun. Warm baths stimulate your circulation. You learn how to share your abundance with others."

Famous People With This Energy Number:

Kobe Bryant, Winona Ryder, Jack Black, and Kim Kardashian

Your Best Direction for <u>Success</u> is <u>North</u>

1/ Soul Journey of Success

Your life will never be boring because you always have your sights set on the future. Some may say you're a perfectionist but you know you're just a professional who's very focused on their career. You're always moving forward, doing the best you can to perfect every step on your path.

An Energy Number 4 is very dedicated to complete what they promised to deliver in a professional field.

If you're a family member of an Energy Number 4, you need to remind them that there needs to be time for rest and relaxation. Finding the balance between a professional life and a family life is a challenge. This number prefers to work alone - you can ask for an office by yourself, but don't forget you also need collaboration and teamwork. You need people around you, otherwise you'll end up taking things too seriously!

2/ Goals for Success

Affirmations share with the Universe your intention for what it is you want to accomplish in your life. But it's not just a message. There's strength in writing these goals in the present tense; you're not demanding or requesting. You're simply telling the Universe what will be. You should never write your affirmations in the future tense as there is great power in stating "This is the way I want my life to be, here and now".

Write down your Success goals on index cards, or place them on your vision board. You can also place them in the North area of your living room, your bedroom, and your office.

Each goal sends your wishes to the Universe, and according to the Law of Attraction, you can attract anything you wish for. Just state your intentions and open yourself up to receive; let the Universe take care of the rest.

If you feel you don't want to place your goals out in the open, you can place them in nice, colored envelopes and address the front to the Universe, God, the Angels, or whomever you are praying to. Remember, Feng Shui is not connected with any specific religion. Instead, it respects all religions and belief systems.

Make your personal Success goals even more powerful by adding:

- An image that represents your goal
- An image of someone (such as a celebrity or someone you know personally) who has already attained a similar goal
- Any symbol that represents your goal

For Example:

You want to be a successful manager in your company and someday retire with great accomplishments. Add images of someone who has been successful in your professional field. Add images of someone walking towards the top of a mountain and put your name on their back.

3/ Quantum Colors for Success

In the Quantum Field, the colors for Success for the Energy Number 4 are **royal blue, cobalt blue,** and **aqua blue.** By placing these colors in the North area of your home and office, you are sending a strong signal to the Universe to activate your Success.

These colors were revealed to me after years of meditation and contemplation, and they are unique to Diamond Feng Shui.

4/ Professional Choices

For you, success and wealth are more likely when you choose the following activities or professional fields:

- Manager or company CEO
- Quality expert
- Police officer or judge
- Safety expert
- Road constructor
- Fisherman or boat maker
- Professional athlete
- Employee for a soft drink, coffee, or tea company

5/ Feng Shui Activations For Your Success in Your Home and Office

1. Facing Direction

During the day, make sure you're facing your Success direction (North) whilst working or meeting up with clients. It's from the North that your strongest Success energy flows. Your ability to attract Success increases greatly when you face towards the North direction whilst you're working, sitting at your desk, looking at your computer screen, when meeting with people, negotiating, and signing contracts.

Avoid sitting with your back to the door since it's poor Feng Shui. From an evolutionary standpoint, our early ancestors faced a lot of dangers in their lives. From wild animals to attacks from other tribes, they had to be completely aware of their surroundings in order to survive. So, from that viewpoint, it makes sense to have a clear view of your door when you're sitting down or in bed so that you know exactly who's coming into the room. If you can't see the door, you make yourself vulnerable to people sneaking up on you.

In terms of Feng Shui, you want to make sure you're in the path of the incoming flow of positive energy. You want to see all the good opportunities that enter through the door, and you want to make sure you're making yourself accessible to any good fortune that comes knocking.

2. Activate Your Personal Success Direction: North

To attract great Success, you need to activate the North area in three places:

- Professional success is focused in the North area of your office
- Personal success is focused in the North area of your living room or family room

- Romantic success is focused in the North area of your bedroom

You can use a compass to find the correct direction. North is between 337.5 and 22.5 degrees on a compass. Make sure you are standing facing the foot end of the bed or couch, or sitting down at your desk when you hold the compass. Similarly, you can use the Diamond Compass on the Marie Diamond app that is connected with your Personal Energy Number.

Next, examine the North area of your office, living room, and bedroom. Do the items, furniture, paintings, and colors represent what you wrote down for your Success goals?

For example, an image of a battlefield can indicate struggle in your career. Make sure there aren't any garbage cans or clutter in the North area because they can block the flow of energy and symbolically put your Success "straight into the garbage".

Use objects that you already have in your home to activate your Success direction. Listed below are several options that will bring good chi to your Success energy:

- Irregular or asymmetric objects
- Glass or transparent objects
- A fountain or an aquarium
- Images of a river or a waterfall

- Blue or black items
- An image of a road
- An image of a white sailboat

In the office, you can also make the space more personal by placing any of the following in your Success direction:

- The logo of your company
- Your products or designs
- Your vision board with your goals
- A personal success affirmation card

Your Best Direction for <u>Health</u> is <u>South</u>

1/ Soul Journey of Health

You need light and warmth to feel happy in your body. Missing your daily portion of time in the sun can make you feel depressed. You love to party but too much of it can impact your immune system, so achieving balance is the key for you. Take dance lessons and surround yourself with music, wear colorful clothing, and display colorful images on your wall. Make sure you have fresh flowers and plants around you. Have fresh, tropical fruit out in a fruit basket.

2/ Goals for Health

Write down your Health goals on index cards, or place them on your vision board. You can also place them in the South area of your living room, your bedroom, and your office.

Each goal sends your wishes to the Universe, and according to the Law of Attraction, you can attract anything you wish for. Just state your intentions and open yourself up to receive; let the Universe take care of the rest.

If you feel you don't want to place your goals out in the open, you can place them in nice, colored envelopes and address the front to the Universe, God, the Angels, or whomever you are praying to. Remember, Feng Shui is not connected with any specific religion. Instead, it respects all religions and belief systems.

Make your personal Health goals even more powerful by adding:

- An image that represents your goal
- An image of someone (such as a celebrity or someone you know personally) who has already attained a similar goal
- Any symbol that represents your goal

The Energy Number Book

For Example:

You want to learn to tango. Add images of a couple doing the tango, where both dancers look healthy and full of life.

3/ Quantum Colors for Health

In the Quantum Field, the colors for Health for the Energy Number 4 are **ruby red**, **cherry red**, and **orange**. By placing these colors in the South area of your home and office, you are sending a strong signal to the Universe to activate your Health.

4/ Health Practices

The following suggestions can help enhance your health energy. These suggestions will not guarantee your health, but instead will make it easier for you to become healthier.

- Keep your body warm and keep a fireplace in your home to snuggle up in front of
- Take special care of your eyes and invest in a pair of high-quality sunglasses
- Take care of your kidneys
- Place images of sunflowers in your health direction
- Place candles around you
- Spend time each day outside in the sun
- Take dance lessons to stay flexible, especially

Latin American dancing
- Express yourself with your voice through singing or acting. A lack of expression can create issues with your throat
- Protect your lungs from smoke-filled environments
- Enjoy the company of enthusiastic people
- Enjoy spicy foods in moderation
- Travel to a warm place once a year

5/ Feng Shui Activations For Your Health in Your Home and Office

1. Facing Direction

When you're in bed, sleep with the top of your head pointing toward your Health direction (South). During the day, sit in your living space or in your dining room facing your health direction.

Your energy level will increase when you sleep with the crown of your head pointing toward this direction, so arrange your bed so you can do so. If you lie on your couch when you're ill, make sure the top of your head faces the South.

2. Activate Your Personal Health Direction: South

To attract good Health, you need to activate the South in three places:

- To stimulate your energy for health when you're working, place Feng Shui activations in the South area of your office. A healthy worker creates a healthy business
- Place Feng Shui activations in the South of your living or family room so that during the daytime, you're creating good energy
- Place Feng Shui activations in the South of your bedroom to stimulate your health whilst you're sleeping and to help you wake up energized in the morning

You can use a compass to find the correct direction. South is between 157.5 and 202.5 degrees on a compass. Make sure you are standing facing the foot end of the bed or couch, or sitting down at your desk when you hold the compass. Similarly, you can use the Diamond Compass on the Marie Diamond app that is connected with your Personal Energy Number.

Next, examine the South area of your office, living room, or bedroom. Do the items, furniture, paintings, and colors represent what you wrote down for your Health goals?

For example, dried flowers in the South are dead items that could attract problems with your immune system. Make sure there aren't any garbage cans or clutter in the South area because they can block the flow of energy and symbolically put your Health "straight into the garbage".

Use objects that you already have in your home to activate your Health direction. Listed below are several options that will bring good chi to your Health energy:

- Objects made of plastic or wood
- Triangle or pyramid-shaped objects, objects with stripes, or long and tall objects
- Images of flowers and plants (but don't use ones with spiky leaves such as cacti, palm trees, or yuccas because they create attacking energy in your living space)
- Real flowers and plants (again, don't use plants with spiky leaves because they pick away at your success)
- Silk flowers and plastic plants (but not dried flowers)
- Fire colors such as red, purple, yellow, orange, rose, fuchsia, brown, beige, and green colored objects
- Magazines and books about show business, art, music, and performance
- Candles
- A Red lamp
- Images of famous musicians, dancers, and singers
- Objects displayed together in groups of nines (such as nine small candles)

You can also make the space more personal by placing any of the following in your Health direction:

- An image of yourself when you appeared radiant and healthy in your living room
- Your vitamins, food supplements, workout or exercise equipment in your bedroom
- Books on health, yoga or relaxation in your office

Your Best Direction for <u>Relationships</u> is <u>East</u>

1/ Soul Journey of Relationships

You view everyone as members of your family. You love to be part of a community and you also enjoy meeting new people who are creative and inventive. You keep family traditions alive and you're the one who keeps track of your family history. Keeping your family together is one of your goals. You're someone who loves to know all the stories from the past and you're a traditionalist in your values for your family.

Even if others think some of your principles are old fashioned, you believe you're taking the best care of your family by respecting these ancient traditions. However, once in a while it's good to open yourself up to modern standards and values. Try to see a way to bridge the old and the new together.

2/ Goals for Relationships

Write down your Relationship goals on index cards, or place them on your vision board. You can also place them in the East area of your living room, your bedroom, and your office.

Each goal sends your wishes to the Universe, and according to the Law of Attraction, you can attract anything you wish for. Just state your intentions and open yourself up to receive; let the Universe take care of the rest.

If you feel you don't want to place your goals out in the open, you can place them in nice, colored envelopes and address the front to the Universe, God, the Angels, or whomever you are praying to. Remember, Feng Shui is not connected with any specific religion. Instead, it respects all religions and belief systems.

Make your personal Relationship goals even more powerful by adding:

- An image that represents your goal
- An image of someone (such as a celebrity or someone you know personally) who has already attained a similar goal
- Any symbol that represents your goal

For Example:

You want to have your entire family together for Christmas in your home. Add pictures of previous holiday family gatherings and write the current year on them.

Special Tip

Single women who want to have a steady romantic relationship should place peonies in their personal relationship direction. They can be real, silk, or just an image. Once you have attracted the relationship you wished for, give the peonies to someone who wishes to have the same kind of luck. Don't keep them. Men can do the same thing but use a bamboo plant instead of peonies.

3/ Quantum Colors for Relationships

In the Quantum Field, the colors for Relationships for Energy Number 4 are **emerald green**, **citrus green**, and **iris blue**. By placing these colors in the East area of your home and office, you are sending a strong signal to the Universe to activate your Relationships.

4/ Relationship Practices

The following are characteristic of those with an Energy Number of 4:

- You work in the family business

- You view your friends as family
- You keep up with your high school and childhood friends
- You enjoy family genealogy
- You save all of the cards and letters that your partner has written to you
- You're interested in the history of your community
- You enjoy walking in the forest with your loved ones
- Your relationship with nature, animals, and plants are important
- You enjoy taking care of newborn babies
- You love playing music with your family and singing along together

5/ Feng Shui Activation For Your Relationships in Your Home and Office

1. Facing Direction

Make sure you sit facing, or sleep with your head pointing towards your relationship direction (East) in order to attract good relationships.

During the day, face the East when you're in the office, attending business meetings, dinners, or important conferences and you will be much more successful with your business relationships.

2. Activate your personal Relationship Direction: East

To attract better relationships, activate the East area in three places:

- For excellent professional relationships, focus on the East area of your office
- For family relationships, focus on the East area of your family or living room
- To stimulate your personal relationship, focus on the East area of your bedroom

You can use a compass to find the correct direction. East is between 67.5 and 112.5 degrees on a compass. Make sure you are standing facing the foot end of the bed or couch, or sitting down at your desk when you hold the compass. Similarly, you can use the Diamond Compass on the Marie Diamond app that is connected with your Personal Energy Number.

Next, examine the East area of your office, living room, or bedroom. Do the items, furniture, paintings, and colors represent what you wrote down for your Relationship goals?

For example, when you have an image of a single flower, don't be surprised if you're not attracting people into your life. Make sure there aren't any garbage cans or clutter in the East area because they can block the flow of energy and symbolically put romance and passion "straight into the garbage".

Use objects that you already have in your home to activate your Relationship direction. Listed below are several options that will bring good chi to your Relationship energy:

- Long and tall objects, or objects with stripes
- Wooden and glass objects
- Antiques
- Flowers and plants
- Images of flowers, plants, forests, and gardens
- Brown and green objects
- Pictures of elders
- Pictures of springtime
- An image of a river or a fountain
- Bamboo wind chimes

You can also make the space more personal by placing any of the following in your Relationship direction:

- In your office, display a photo of your professional team, or of you and your manager. Also, place your address book or business cards from your clients in the East area
- In your living or family room, display recent photos of you with your loved ones. Also, photos of you and your friends
- In your bedroom, place photos of you with your romantic partner. Photos of you with your children can work here too, but not of you with your mother-in-law

Your Best Direction for <u>Wisdom</u> is <u>Southeast</u>

1/ Soul Journey of Wisdom

You will learn your spiritual lessons by working with money. Others come to you for financial advice because you know how to practice and teach success principles. That would be the ultimate version of the wisdom path of the Energy Number 4 but there is often a long journey they will need to walk before this manifests. Understand that money is manna - it's created by God as a vehicle to understand the manifestation of power in you. Once you understand the universal principles behind money, you will reach enlightenment

2/ Goals for Wisdom

Write down your Wisdom goals on index cards, or place them on your vision board. You can also place them in the Southeast area of your living room, your bedroom, and your office.

Each goal sends your wishes to the Universe, and according to the Law of Attraction, you can attract anything you wish for. Just state your intentions and open yourself up to receive; let the Universe take care of the rest. If you feel you don't want to place your goals out in the open, you can place them in nice, colored envelopes and address the front to the Universe, God, the Angels, or whomever you are praying to. Remember, Feng Shui is not connected with any specific religion. Instead, it respects all religions and belief systems.

Make your personal Wisdom goals even more powerful by adding:

- An image that represents your goal
- An image of someone (such as a celebrity or someone you know personally) who has already attained a similar goal
- Any symbol that represents your goal

For Example:

You want to teach your children spiritual abundance. Place books about spiritual abundance next to your children's pictures.

3/ Quantum Colors for Wisdom

In the Quantum Field, the colors for Wisdom for Energy Number 4 are **violet**, **lilac**, and **gold**. By placing these colors in the Southeast area of your home and office, you are sending a strong signal to the Universe to activate your Wisdom.

4/ Wisdom Practices

You receive knowledge and wisdom most effectively by:
- Studying wealthy men and women
- Taking self-improvement courses

- Learning more about financial management
- Working in your garden with plants and flowers
- Becoming a philanthropist and donating to charity
- Having a more spiritual approach to money
- Helping to improve the good fortune of the world
- Giving to the homeless

5/ Feng Shui Activations For Your Wisdom in Your Home and Office

1. Facing Direction

When seeking knowledge or spiritual awareness, sit facing your Wisdom direction (Southeast). It's from the Southeast that your strongest Wisdom energy flows. You will attract greater wisdom and knowledge if you face the Southeast whilst you're studying, at your desk, meditating, or praying.

2. Activate Your Personal Wisdom Direction: Southeast

To attract great Wisdom, you need to activate the Southeast areas in three places:

- Stimulate your professional wisdom by placing Feng Shui activations in the Southeast area of your office
- Stimulate your social Wisdom by placing Feng

Shui activations in the Southeast of your living or family room
- Stimulate your nightly insights by placing Feng Shui activations in the Southeast of your bedroom

You can use a compass to find the correct direction. Southeast is between 112.5 and 157.5 degrees on a compass. Make sure you are standing facing the foot end of the bed or couch, or sitting down at your desk when you hold the compass. Similarly, you can use the Diamond Compass on the Marie Diamond app that is connected with your Personal Energy Number.

Next, examine the Southeast area of your office, living room, or bedroom. Do the items, furniture, paintings, and colors represent what you wrote down for your Wisdom goals? For example, an image of a homeless person here would show the Universe that you are not at home in your own spirit. Make sure there aren't any garbage cans or clutter in the Southeast area because they can block the flow of energy and symbolically put your Wisdom "straight into the garbage".

Use objects that you already have in your home to activate your Wisdom area. Listed below are several options that will bring good chi to your Wisdom energy:

- Cylindrical shaped objects, objects with stripes, and long, tall objects

- Objects made of wood
- Brown, beige, green and lilac-colored objects
- A small fountain
- Silk flowers and plastic plants (but not dried flowers)
- A wealth ship, a money frog, or a bowl with coins
- Real flowers and plants (avoid plants with spiky leaves because they pick away at your success)
- Images of flowers and plants (but do not use plants with spiky leaves such as cactus, palm trees, or yuccas because they create attacking energy)
- Magazines and books on financial advice or on creating wealth and money
- Images of spiritual or religious millionaires
- An image of a small waterfall or of a river in a green, lush landscape

You can also make the space more personal by placing any of the following in your Wisdom direction:

- In your living room, an image of your church or spiritual community.
- In your office, quotes from enlightened businessmen or books on business ethics
- In your bedroom, a bible or any meditation tools

Your Vision Board

When you make a vision board, it helps to think of it as a map. The difference is that at the top of your board always represents the South and the bottom always represents the North. In order to make a vision board that creates the best results with the Law of Attraction, place a photo of you in the center and fill the vision board with the following outline:

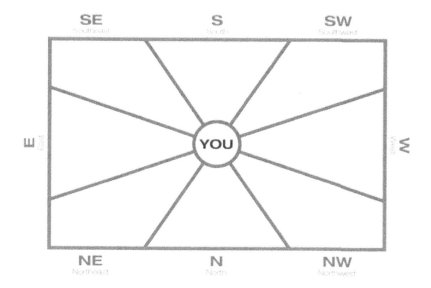

Your Success Direction

In the bottom center: North
- Write down your Success goals
- Activate it with Success images
- Activate it with the color royal blue and your quantum colors for Success

Your Health Direction

In the top center: South
- Write down your Health goals
- Activate it with Health images
- Activate it with the color emerald green and your quantum colors for Health

Your Relationship Direction

In the center left: East
- Write down your Relationship goals
- Activate it with Relationship images
- Activate it with the color rose and your quantum colors for relationships

Your Wisdom Direction

In the upper left corner: Southeast
- Write down your Wisdom goals
- Activate it with Wisdom images
- Activate it with the color yellow and your quantum colors for Wisdom

The Rest of Your Vision Board

You can fill up the rest of your vision board with images that relate to more general areas of Feng Shui, such as:
- Southwest: Romance, feminine energy, and motherhood

- West: Creativity, communication, and children
- Northwest: Travel, advisors, friends, and space
- Northeast: Wisdom, spirituality, and knowledge
- Center: Harmony and balance

Every year, the background colors for the Vision Board change in accordance with the Yearly Law of Attraction based on Diamond Time Feng Shui.

Look for the most current Diamond Vision Board Poster, and for other Marie Diamond Feng Shui products at: http://mariediamond.com

CHAPTER 5
Energy Number 5 (Man): The Teacher

Go to Chapter 2, Energy Number 2: The Teacher

It Has the Same Information as Energy Number 5 (Man)

CHAPTER 6
Energy Number 5 (Woman): The Connector

Go to Chapter 9, Energy Number 8: The Connector

It Has the Same Information as Energy Number 5 (Woman)

CHAPTER 7
Energy Number 6:
The Creator

Introduction

The Energy Archetype connected with Energy Number 6 is called the **Creator**. The essence of the Creator is:

"You are a creative thinker and innovator in both your professional and personal life. You are a fan of new technologies and love to have the latest gadgets. To you, women are Goddesses and you relate better to women than to men. You are always ready to help others grow to be better human beings and in your circle of friends your wisdom is appreciated."

Famous People With This Energy Number:

Guy Fieri, Meryl Streep, Justin Bieber, and Kamala Harris

Your Best Direction for <u>Success</u> is <u>West</u>

1/ Soul Journey of Success

You will create success by following your intuition and by using your innovative ideas and creativity. Be open to using new technologies to create wealth. You can amass wealth more quickly by working with products aimed at children and teenagers, high-tech products, or products that are cost-effective to produce and have a wide appeal. However, you'll need to accept that at the beginning, people won't always appreciate your value. Keep focused on your new innovative ideas and continue to move forward.

2/ Goals for Success

Affirmations share with the Universe your intention for what it is you want to accomplish in your life. But it's not just a message. There's strength in writing these goals in the present tense; you're not demanding or requesting. You're simply telling the Universe what will be. You should never write your affirmations in the future tense as there is great power in stating "This is the way I want my life to be, here and now".

Write down your Success goals on index cards, or place them on your vision board. You can also place them in the West area of your living room, your bedroom, and your office.

Each goal sends your wishes to the Universe, and according to the Law of Attraction, you can attract anything you wish for. Just state your intentions and open yourself up to receive; let the Universe take care of the rest.

If you feel you don't want to place your goals out in the open, you can place them in nice, colored envelopes and address the front to the Universe, God, the Angels, or whomever you are praying to. Remember, Feng Shui is not connected with any specific religion. Instead, it respects all religions and belief systems.

Make your personal Success goals even more powerful by adding:

- An image that represents your goal
- An image of someone (such as a celebrity or someone you know personally) who has already attained a similar goal
- Any symbol that represents your goal

For Example:

You wish to become very successful with your new website or app idea and sell it to a big company. Add images of a company or the logo of a website that has already achieved this. Add images of money like a fake million dollar bill, or images of a millionaire lifestyle such as a large mansion, a private jet, a yacht, or expensive watches.

3/ Quantum Colors for Success

In the Quantum Field, the colors for Success for the Energy Number 6 are **white**, **ivory white**, and **peach**. By placing these colors in the West area of your home and office, you are sending a strong signal to the Universe to activate your Success.

These colors were revealed to me after years of meditation and contemplation, and they are unique to Diamond Feng Shui.

4/ Professional Choices

For you, success and wealth are more likely when you choose the following activities or professional fields:

- Creating, selling, or marketing new inspiring products, concepts, or companies
- Internet, technology, or communications
- Stocks and bonds investment
- Coaching and personal consultation
- Psychologist or psychiatrist specializing in trauma relief, or in children or family therapy
- Working for a toy, candy, or sweet company
- Child Care and Teaching
- Marketing
- Entertainment

5/ Feng Shui Activations For Your Success in Your Home and Office

1. Facing Direction

During the day, make sure you're facing your Success direction (West) whilst working or meeting up with clients. It's from the West that your strongest Success energy flows. Your ability to attract Success increases greatly when you face the West whilst you're working, sitting at your desk, looking at your computer screen, when meeting with people, negotiating, and signing contracts.

Avoid sitting with your back to the door since it's poor Feng Shui. From an evolutionary standpoint, our early ancestors faced a lot of dangers in their lives. From wild animals to attacks from other tribes, they had to be completely aware of their surroundings in order to survive. So, from that viewpoint, it makes sense to have a clear view of your door when you're sitting down or in bed so that you know exactly who's coming into the room. If you can't see the door, you make yourself vulnerable to people sneaking up on you.

In terms of Feng Shui, you want to make sure you're in the path of the incoming flow of positive energy. You want to see all the good opportunities that enter through the door, and you want to make sure you're making yourself accessible to any good fortune that comes knocking.

2. Activate Your Personal Success Direction: West

To attract great Success, you need to activate the West area in three places:

- Professional success is focused in the West area of your office
- Personal success is focused in the West area of your living room or family room
- Romantic success is focused in the West area of your bedroom

You can use a compass to find the correct direction. West is between 247.5 and 292.5 degrees on a compass. Make sure you are standing facing the foot end of the bed or couch, or sitting down at your desk when you hold the compass. Similarly, you can use the Diamond Compass on the Marie Diamond app that is connected with your Personal Energy Number.

Next, examine the West area of your office, living room, and bedroom. Do the items, furniture, paintings, and colors represent what you wrote down for your Success goals?

For example, if you have a painting of a sinking ship, is this representative of a good career? Make sure there aren't any garbage cans or clutter in the West area because they can block the flow of energy and symbolically put your Success "straight into the garbage".

Use objects that you already have in your home to activate your Success direction. Listed below are several options that will bring good chi to your Success energy:

- Metal or metal-colored objects
- White or gray objects
- Ceramics or crystal
- Metal wind chimes (a six or seven rod that is metal and hollow is best)
- Gemstones

- Artwork or crafts
- Playful objects, toys, and gadgets
- Image of a deep lake or ocean
- Image of sailing boats
- Technical tools or images
- Stereo, records, or CDs
- Television
- Objects associated with wind such as flags or wind makers
- Round or oval objects

In the office, you can also make the space more personal by placing any of the following in your Success direction:

- The logo of your company
- Your products or designs
- Your vision board with your goals
- A personal success affirmation card
- Pictures of your family or photos from the latest family trip

Your Best Direction for <u>Health</u> is <u>Northeast</u>

1/ Soul Journey of Health

Creating better health is more likely to occur when you take care of yourself. Learn to relax and find inner peace and happiness with daily prayer, reflection, meditation, or reading from an inspiring book. This will improve your mental and emotional health, and ultimately your physical health as well. Taking care of your hands will improve your total body energy. Massage is a must for you to help relieve tension and reconnect you with your body.

The Energy Number 6 needs to learn to enjoy their own inner peace by listening to their inner voice. They tend to be too focused on analyzing their health and not enough on trusting their intuition. If your inner voice tells you that you need rest, just take it and don't analyze the pros and cons of doing so.

2/ Goals for Health

Write down your Health goals on index cards, or place them on your vision board. You can also place them in the Northeast area of your living room, your bedroom, and your office.

Each goal sends your wishes to the Universe, and according to the Law of Attraction, you can attract anything you wish for. Just state your intentions and open yourself up to receive; let the Universe take care of the rest.

If you feel you don't want to place your goals out in the open, you can place them in nice, colored envelopes and address the front to the Universe, God, the Angels, or whomever you are praying to. Remember, Feng Shui is not connected with any specific religion. Instead, it respects all religions and belief systems.

Make your personal Health goals even more powerful by adding:

- An image that represents your goal
- An image of someone (such as a celebrity or someone you know personally) who has already attained a similar goal
- Any symbol that represents your goal

For Example:

You want to meditate every morning and evening. Add images of a Tibetan monk praying at sunrise.

3/ Quantum Colors for Health

In the Quantum Field, the colors for Health for the Energy Number 6 are **yellow, saffron yellow,** and **magenta**. By placing these colors in the Northeast area of your home and office, you are sending a strong signal to the Universe to activate your Health.

4/ Health Practices

The following suggestions can help enhance your health energy. These suggestions will not guarantee your health, but instead will make it easier for you to become healthier.

- Focus on maintaining balance and peace in your life
- Read books and do research on healthy living

- Connect with people who have knowledge and wisdom about the physical issues you're facing
- Take time daily to meditate or to pray. Face the Northeast direction when you do this
- Have a regular manicure. Healthy hands mean a healthy body for you
- See a psychologist to search for any emotional or mental factors behind your health issues
- Let go of a secret you're holding on to
- Live more like a monk and limit any excessive behaviors
- Forgive yourself for past behaviors

5/ Feng Shui Activations For Your Health in Your Home and Office

1. Facing Direction

When you're in bed, sleep with the top of your head pointing toward your Health direction (Northeast). During the day, sit in your living space or in your dining room facing your Health direction.

Your energy level will increase when you sleep with the crown of your head pointing toward this direction, so arrange your bed so you can do so. If you lie on your couch when you're ill, make sure the top of your head faces the Northeast.

2. *Activate Your Personal Health Direction: Northeast*

To attract good health, you need to activate the Northeast in three places:

- To stimulate your energy for health when you're working, place Feng Shui activations in the Northeast area of your office. A healthy worker creates a healthy business
- Place Feng Shui activations in the Northeast of your living or family room so that during the daytime, you're creating good energy.
- Place Feng Shui activations in the Northeast of your bedroom to stimulate your health whilst you're sleeping and to help you wake up energized in the morning

You can use a compass to find the correct direction. Northeast is between 22.5 and 67.5 degrees on a compass. Make sure you are standing facing the foot end of the bed or couch, or sitting down at your desk when you hold the compass. Similarly, you can use the Diamond Compass on the Marie Diamond app that is connected with your Personal Energy Number.

Next, examine the Northeast area of your office, living room, or bedroom. Do the items, furniture, paintings, and colors represent what you wrote down for your Health goals?

For example, if you have a Greek statue without arms and hands, don't be surprised if you have problems with your own bone structure. Make sure there aren't any garbage cans or clutter in the Northeast area because they can block the flow of energy and symbolically put your Health "straight into the garbage".

Use objects that you already have in your home to activate your Health direction. Listed below are several options that will bring good chi to your Health energy:

- Square or cubical objects
- Ceramic or crystal objects
- Meditating Buddha statue
- Images and statues of Gods, Goddesses, Saints, or Angels
- Beige, orange, yellow, turquoise, red, rose, or purple objects
- Books on health
- Pictures of athletes running a marathon
- Image of a mountain (Make sure it's not completely covered in snow)
- Lotus flowers
- Candles, incense, and lamps
- Gemstones

You can also make the space more personal by placing any of the following in your Health direction:

- An image of yourself when you appeared radiant and healthy in your living room
- Your vitamins, food supplements, workout or exercise equipment in your bedroom
- Books on health, yoga or relaxation in your office

Your Best Direction for <u>Relationships</u> is <u>Southwest</u>

1/ Soul Journey of Relationships

Romance for you is only possible with someone who is your best friend. You and your loved ones are like a team, together through good and bad times. You're a romantic soul and are looking for your knight in shining armor. Taking quality time for your children and other family members is important for you. Hosting and cooking for others is your natural way of connecting.

The only thing an Energy Number 6 needs to be aware of is that you don't have to take care of the whole world. You can only do your part and you need to let others take care of you too.

2/ Goals for Relationships

Write down your Relationship goals on index cards, or place them on your vision board. You can also place them in the Southwest area of your living room, your bedroom, and your office.

Each goal sends your wishes to the Universe, and according to the Law of Attraction, you can attract anything you wish for. Just state your intentions and open yourself up to receive; let the Universe take care of the rest.

If you feel you don't want to place your goals out in the open, you can place them in nice, colored envelopes and address the front to the Universe, God, the Angels, or whomever you are praying to. Remember, Feng Shui is not connected with any specific religion. Instead, it respects all religions and belief systems.

Make your personal Relationship goals even more powerful by adding:

- An image that represents your goal
- An image of someone (such as a celebrity or someone you know personally) who has already attained a similar goal
- Any symbol that represents your goal

For Example:

You wish to attract a great team to collaborate with. Add images of a successful team that won a championship.

Special Tip

Single women who want to have a steady romantic relationship should place peonies in their personal relationship direction. They can be real, silk, or just an image. Once you have attracted the relationship you wished for, give the peonies to someone who wishes to have the same kind of luck. Don't keep them. Men can do the same thing but use a bamboo plant instead of peonies.

3/ Quantum Colors for Relationships

In the Quantum Field, the colors for Relationships for Energy Number 6 are **rose**, **pink**, and **fuchsia**. By placing these colors in the Southwest area of your home and office, you are sending a strong signal to the Universe to activate your Relationships.

4/ Relationship Practices

The following are characteristic of those with an Energy Number of 6:

- You like to mother your partner and other people around you. It's possible that you live with your mother, or honor her above your romantic partner
- You love to work with women and teaming up with them gives you a lot of inspiration
- You love collaboration
- You love going on adventures with your loved

ones and have a special interest for native cultures

- You connect with people from all over the world
- You love spending time with your partner hiking in the mountains
- You may attract older romantic partners that you can take care of
- You believe in a knight in the shining armor on a white horse. Fairy tales and love stories give you an idealistic view on relationships
- The body part that receives the most attention in romance are your breasts
- You may attract partners that are looking more for a mother than a partner
- Your purpose for relationships is to focus on romance, collaboration, and tenderness
- You make food for everyone that comes to your home
- Invite friends out for dinner, go with your family on a trip, or have candlelit dinners at home
- Connect with local people in your own town or on your travels
- Connect with the power of gemstones and put incense or candles out to create a romantic living room.

5/ Feng Shui Activations For Your Relationships in Your Home and Office

1. Facing Direction

Make sure you sit facing, or sleep with your head pointing towards your Relationship direction (Southwest) in order to attract good relationships.

During the day, face the Southwest when you're in the office, attending business meetings, dinners, or important conferences and you will be much more successful with your business relationships.

2. Activate Your Personal Relationship Direction: Southwest

To attract better relationships, activate the Southwest area in three places:

- For excellent professional relationships, focus on the Southwest area of your office
- For family relationships, focus on the Southwest area of your family or living room
- To stimulate your personal relationship, focus on the Southwest area of your bedroom

You can use a compass to find the correct direction. Southwest is between 202.5 and 247.5 degrees on a compass. Make sure you are standing facing the foot end of the bed or couch, or sitting down at your desk when you hold the compass. Similarly, you can use the

Diamond Compass on the Marie Diamond app that is connected with your Personal Energy Number.

Next, examine the Southwest area of your office, living room, or bedroom. Do the items, furniture, paintings, and colors represent what you wrote down for your Relationship goals?

For example, if you have images of women standing alone, don't be surprised if you find yourself alone as a woman. Make sure there aren't any garbage cans or clutter in the Southwest area because they can block the flow of energy and symbolically put romance and passion "straight into the garbage".

Use objects that you already have in your home to activate your relationship direction. Listed below are several options that will bring good chi to your Relationship energy:

- Square or cubical objects
- Ceramics or crystal objects
- Two rose quartz hearts that are touching
- Items grouped together in pairs
- The double happiness symbol
- Love birds
- A pair of mandarin ducks connected with a red ribbon
- Images of romantic couples with lasting relationships
- Images of a team playing together and having

fun
- A ceramic friendship circle
- Images of a compassionate mother, like Kuan Yin or Lady Mary
- Two red or rose candles

You can also make the space more personal by placing any of the following in your Relationship direction:

- In your office, display a photo of your professional team, or of you and your manager. Also, place your address book or business cards from your clients in the Southwest area
- In your living or family room, display recent photos of you with your loved ones. Also, photos of you and your friends
- In your bedroom, place photos of you with your romantic partner. Photos of you with your children can work here too, but not of you with your mother-in-law

Your Best Direction for <u>Wisdom</u> is <u>Northwest</u>

1/ Soul Journey of Wisdom

You stimulate your knowledge by studying other cultures and countries. You learn a lot through traveling. Having a mentor or a coach will bring you new perspectives in your personal life. Read your daily astrology or use numerology to help you to understand your life better. Stargazing will also inspire you. Advising others will help you to improve your own wisdom. People will more readily accept your wisdom when you are fifty years old or older.

2/ Goals for Wisdom

Write down your Wisdom goals on index cards, or place them on your vision board. You can also place them in the Northwest area of your living room, your bedroom, and your office.

Each goal sends your wishes to the Universe, and according to the Law of Attraction, you can attract anything you wish for. Just state your intentions and open yourself up to receive; let the Universe take care of the rest.

If you feel you don't want to place your goals out in the open, you can place them in nice, colored envelopes and address the front to the Universe, God, the Angels, or whomever you are praying to. Remember, Feng Shui is not connected with any specific religion. Instead, it respects all religions and belief systems.

Make your personal Wisdom goals even more powerful by adding:

- An image that represents your goal
- An image of someone (such as a celebrity or someone you know personally) who has already attained a similar goal

- Any symbol that represents your goal

For Example:

You wish to have more time connecting with God. Add images of someone who is praying. You can add images of a spiritual or religious leader who is an example of devotion.

3/ Quantum Colors for Wisdom

In the Quantum Field, the colors for Wisdom for Energy Number 6 are **opal**, **diamond**, and **silver**. By placing these colors in the Northwest area of your home and office, you are sending a strong signal to the Universe to activate your Wisdom.

4/ Wisdom Practices

You receive knowledge and wisdom most effectively by:

- Connecting with older male coaches and mentors
- Listening to the wisdom of your grandfather, father, or the elder men of your community or church
- Astronomy can be a great source of wisdom for you
- Anything connected with oracles, astrology, tarot, or divination
- Giving advice to other people looking for

answers for their own life questions
- Gazing at the stars
- Traveling to new places
- Seeking advice from professional coaches

5/ Feng Shui Activations For Your Wisdom in Your Home and Office

1. Facing Direction

When seeking knowledge or spiritual awareness, sit facing your Wisdom direction (Northwest). It's from the Northwest that your strongest Wisdom energy flows. You will attract greater wisdom and knowledge if you face the Northwest whilst you're studying, at your desk, meditating, or praying.

2. Activate Your Personal Wisdom Direction: Northwest

To attract great Wisdom, you need to activate the Northwest areas of three places:

- Stimulate your professional wisdom by placing Feng Shui activations in the Northwest area of your office
- Stimulate your social Wisdom by placing Feng Shui activations in the Northwest of your living or family room
- Stimulate your nightly insights by placing Feng Shui activations in the Northwest of your bedroom

You can use a compass to find the correct direction. Northwest is between 292.5 and 337.5 degrees on a compass. Make sure you are standing facing the foot end of the bed or couch, or sitting down at your desk when you hold the compass. Similarly, you can use the Diamond Compass on the Marie Diamond app that is connected with your Personal Energy Number.

Next, examine the Northwest area of your office, living room, or bedroom. Do the items, furniture, paintings, and colors represent what you wrote down for your Wisdom goals?

For example, you have a statue of someone sitting with his head between his hands looking down and depressed. Do you think this depressed person is open to God and the Universe? Make sure there aren't any garbage cans or clutter in the Northwest area because they can block the flow of energy and symbolically put your Wisdom "straight into the garbage".

Use objects that you already have in your home to activate your Wisdom area. Listed below are several options that will bring good chi to your Wisdom energy:

- Round or oval objects
- Metal or metal-colored objects
- Images of stars, the moon, and the planets
- Images of wise men like Einstein
- Image of Jesus, Buddha, or other holy men

- Images of Saints, Angels, or spiritual and religious leaders
- White or gray objects
- Metal wind chimes (six-rods with hollow metal tubes are best)
- Gemstones like citrine geodes

You can also make the space more personal by placing any of the following in your Wisdom direction:

- In your living room, an image of your church or spiritual community.
- In your office, quotes from enlightened businessmen or books on business ethics
- In your bedroom, a bible or any meditation tools

Your Vision Board

When you make a vision board, it helps to think of it as a map. The difference is that at the top of your board always represents the South and the bottom always represents the North.

In order to make a vision board that creates the best results with the Law of Attraction, place a photo of you in the center and fill the vision board with the following outline:

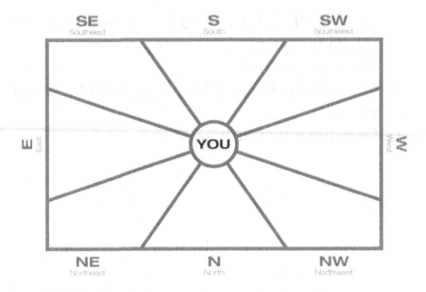

Your Success Direction

In the center of the right: West
- Write down your Success goals
- Activate it with Success images
- Activate it with the color royal blue and your quantum colors for Success

Your Health Direction

In the left bottom corner: Northeast
- Write down your Health goals
- Activate it with Health images
- Activate it with the color emerald green and your quantum colors for Health

Your Relationship Direction

In the upper right corner: Southwest
- Write down your Relationship goals
- Activate it with Relationship images
- Activate it with the color rose and your quantum colors for relationships

Your Wisdom Direction

In the right bottom corner: Northwest
- Write down your Wisdom goals
- Activate it with Wisdom images
- Activate it with the color yellow and your quantum colors for Wisdom

The Rest of Your Vision Board

You can fill up the rest of your vision board with images that relate to more general areas of Feng Shui, such as:

- South: Self Esteem, entertainment, enlightenment, and dance
- North: Career and journey
- East: Family, health, government, elders, and the past
- Southeast: Money, luxury, and good fortune
- Center: Harmony and balance

Every year, the background colors for the Vision Board change in accordance with the Yearly Law of Attraction based on Diamond Time Feng Shui.

Look for the most current Diamond Vision Board Poster, and for other Marie Diamond Feng Shui products at: http://mariediamond.com

CHAPTER 8
Energy Number 7:
The Advisor

Introduction

The Energy Archetype connected with Energy Number 7 is called the **Advisor**. The essence of the Advisor is:

"Your focus is on the highest good for all, and you have the ability to express this ideology to everyone you are involved with. Your health is improved by nurturing yourself. In your relationships, you honor the talents of others and help them progress to the next level. Children are a source of constant inspiration for you."

Famous People With This Energy Number:

Tiger Woods, Gordon Ramsey, David Beckham, and Billie Eilish

Your Best Direction for <u>Success</u> is <u>Northwest</u>

1/ Soul Journey of Success

When creating your Success, the support of your friends and family is crucial. You may be in business with people from other countries or like to work with products from other cultures. Networking is natural for you. You likely have a coach or mentor advising you in your professional life. You are a natural leader and people will look to you for leadership. It's your choice whether or not to take on this role.

2/ Goals for Success

Affirmations share with the Universe your intention for what it is you want to accomplish in your life. But it's not just a message. There's strength in writing these goals in the present tense; you're not demanding or requesting. You're simply telling the Universe what will be. You should never write your affirmations in the future tense as there is great power in stating "This is the way I want my life to be, here and now".

Write down your Success goals on index cards, or place them on your vision board. You can also place them in the Northwest area of your living room, your bedroom, and your office.

Each goal sends your wishes to the Universe, and according to the Law of Attraction, you can attract anything you wish for. Just state your intentions and open yourself up to receive; let the Universe take care of the rest.

If you feel you don't want to place your goals out in the open, you can place them in nice, colored envelopes and address the front to the Universe, God, the Angels, or whomever you are praying to. Remember, Feng Shui is not connected with any specific religion. Instead, it respects all religions and belief systems.

Make your personal Success goals even more powerful by adding:

- An image that represents your goal
- An image of someone (such as a celebrity or someone you know personally) who has already attained a similar goal
- Any symbol that represents your goal

For Example:

You wish to become a multi-millionaire, one who is considered as a "good father" to the community. You add images of a well-known person who has already accomplished this goal, such as Bill Gates. Add images of money like a fake billion-dollar bill, or what you wish to have when you are a multi-millionaire such as a large mansion, a private jet, a yacht, or a golden watch.

3/ Quantum Colors for Success

In the Quantum Field, the colors for Success for the Energy Number 7 are **opal**, **diamond**, and **silver**. By placing these colors in the Northwest area of your home and office, you are sending a strong signal to the Universe to activate your Success.

These colors were revealed to me after years of meditation and contemplation, and they are unique to Diamond Feng Shui.

4/ Professional Choices

For you, success and wealth are more likely when you choose the following activities or professional fields:

- Space engineer, pilot, or a job involving airplanes
- Consultant, coach, or networker
- CEO of a company
- Working with your friends, your father or elder men in your business
- Work investing in gold and silver
- Working with metal objects or a job involving cars
- TV or radio show host
- Travel agent
- Mathematics teacher

5/ Feng Shui Activations For Your Success in your Home and Office

1. Facing Direction

During the day, make sure you're facing your Success direction (Northwest) whilst working or meeting up with clients. It's from the Northwest that your strongest Success energy flows. Your ability to attract Success increases greatly when you face towards the Northwest direction whilst you're working, sitting at your desk, looking at your computer screen, when meeting with people, negotiating, and signing contracts.

Avoid sitting with your back to the door since it's poor Feng Shui. From an evolutionary standpoint, our early ancestors faced a lot of dangers in their lives. From wild animals to attacks from other tribes, they had to be completely aware of their surroundings in order to survive. So, from that viewpoint, it makes sense to have a clear view of your door when you're sitting down or in bed so that you know exactly who's coming into the room. If you can't see the door, you make yourself vulnerable to people sneaking up on you. In terms of Feng Shui, you want to make sure you're in the path of the incoming flow of positive energy. You want to see all the good opportunities that enter through the door, and you want to make sure you're making yourself accessible to any good fortune that comes knocking.

2. Activate Your Personal Success Direction: Northwest

To attract great Success, you need to activate the Northwest area in three places:

- Professional success is focused in the Northwest area of your office
- Personal success is focused in the Northwest area of your living room or family room
- Romantic success is focused in the Northwest area of your bedroom

You can use a compass to find the correct direction. Northwest is between 292.5 and 337.5 degrees on a compass. Make sure you are standing facing the foot end of the bed or couch, or sitting down at your desk when you hold the compass. Similarly, you can use the Diamond Compass on the Marie Diamond app that is connected with your Personal Energy Number.

Next, examine the Northwest area of your office, living room, and bedroom. Do the items, furniture, paintings, and colors represent what you wrote down for your Success goals?

For example, if you have a painting of a sinking ship, is this representative of an exceptional career? Make sure there aren't any garbage cans or clutter in the Northwest area because they can block the flow of energy and symbolically put your Success "straight into the garbage".

Use objects that you already have in your home to activate your Success direction. Listed below are several options that will bring good chi to your Success energy:

- Round or oval objects
- Metal or metal-colored objects
- White objects
- Ceramics or crystal objects
- Images of your father and you, or you as a father

- Images of you with your children
- Images of space, the moon, stars, and planets
- Metal wind chimes (six rods with hollow, metal tubes is best)
- Gemstones
- Images of your mentors or coach, presidents, wise men, spiritual teachers, or religious leaders
- Images of angels or fairies
- Books on success or about successful people

In the office, you can also make the space more personal by placing any of the following in your Success direction:

- The logo of your company
- Your products or designs
- Your vision board with your goals
- A personal success affirmation card

Your Best Direction for <u>Health</u> is <u>Southwest</u>

1/ Soul Journey of Health

Creating great health requires taking care of yourself and having a balanced diet. It's important to always take care of your organs because this will be a weak point for you. Do a regular detoxing program for your organs and intestines. Let yourself be mothered and nurtured by a loved one. Your health situation is more likely to influence your personal relationships, so don't complain too much about your health. Falling in love with your health practitioner could be good for your health!

2/ Goals for Health

Write down your Health goals on index cards, or place them on your vision board. You can also place them in the Southwest area of your living room, your bedroom, and your office.

Each goal sends your wishes to the Universe, and according to the Law of Attraction, you can attract anything you wish for. Just state your intentions and open yourself up to receive; let the Universe take care of the rest.

If you feel you don't want to place your goals out in the open, you can place them in nice, colored envelopes and address the front to the Universe, God, the Angels, or whomever you are praying to. Remember, Feng Shui is not connected with any specific religion. Instead, it respects all religions and belief systems.

Make your personal Health goals even more powerful by adding:

- An image that represents your goal
- An image of someone (such as a celebrity or someone you know personally) who has already attained a similar goal

- Any symbol that represents your goal

For Example:

When you want to lose weight, add images of someone who has lost a substantial amount and looks great, such as Oprah Winfrey. You can add the number of pounds you want to lose or the clothing size you wish to be.

3/ Quantum Colors for Health

In the Quantum Field, the colors for Health for the Energy Number 7 are **rose**, **pink**, and **fuchsia**. By placing these colors in the Southwest area of your home and office, you are sending a strong signal to the Universe for activating your Health.

4/ Health Practices

The following suggestions can help enhance your health energy. These suggestions will not guarantee your health, but instead will make it easier for you to become healthier.

- Get enough sleep and drink enough water every day
- Focus on nutrition and learn how to cook healthy meals
- Detoxify yourself every few months, or do a juice fast
- Eat vegetables that are from the root family,

potatoes in particular will strengthen you
- Collaborate with others to keep yourself from taking on too much by yourself
- Take extra care of your romantic life because any challenges there can affect your health
- Let your mother take care of you
- Indulge in mud baths or in a mud wrap at a spa

5/ Feng Shui Activations For Your Health in Your Home and Office

1. Facing Direction

When you're in bed, sleep with the top of your head pointing toward your Health direction (Southwest). During the day, sit in your living space or in your dining room facing your health direction.

Your energy level will increase when you sleep with the crown of your head pointing toward this direction, so arrange your bed so you can do so. If you lie on your couch when you're ill, make sure the top of your head faces the Southwest.

2. Activate Your Personal Health Direction: Southwest

To attract good Health, you need to activate the Southwest in three places:

- To stimulate your energy for health when you're working, place Feng Shui activations in the Southwest area of your office. A healthy worker creates a healthy business

- Place Feng Shui activations in the Southwest of your living or family room so that during the daytime, you're creating good energy
- Place Feng Shui activations in the Southwest of your bedroom to stimulate your health whilst you're sleeping and to help you wake up energized in the morning

You can use a compass to find the correct direction. Southwest is between 202.5 and 247.5 degrees on a compass. Make sure you are standing facing the foot end of the bed or couch, or sitting down at your desk when you hold the compass. Similarly, you can use the Diamond Compass on the Marie Diamond app that is connected with your Personal Energy Number.

Next, examine the Southwest area of your office, living room, or bedroom. Do the items, furniture, paintings, and colors represent what you wrote down for your Health goals?

For example, an image of a desert could attract poor immunity. Make sure there aren't any garbage cans or clutter in the Southwest area because they can block the flow of energy and symbolically put your Health "straight into the garbage".

Use objects that you already have in your home to activate your Health direction. Listed below are several options that will bring good chi to your Health energy:

- Square or cubical objects
- Ceramic or crystal objects
- A large rose quartz heart
- Items grouped together in pairs
- The double happiness symbol
- A crystal globe
- Two red or rose candles
- An image of a compassionate mother, like Kuan Yin or Lady Mary
- An image of a mother and a baby animal
- An image that represents nurturing

You can also make the space more personal by placing any of the following in your Health direction:

- An image of yourself when you appeared radiant and healthy in your living room
- Your vitamins, food supplements, workout or exercise equipment in your bedroom
- Books on health, yoga or relaxation in your office

Your Best Direction for Relationships is Northeast

1/ Soul Journey of Relationships

You love sharing your knowledge and wisdom with others and you're a natural teacher. Taking part in spiritual or religious practices with your loved ones benefits your relationships. Traveling with family and friends, going on guided tours, and learning more about other cultures are all highlights in your life.

For you, balance and peace are essentials for a great romance. Anyone who can create this for you is definitely a person you'd like to be with for the rest of your life. However, you need to learn to listen to your own inner guidance and not always rely on others for intuition and knowledge. When you're older, you'll start to understand that your wisdom is as valuable as someone else's.

2/ Goals for Relationships

Write down your Relationship goals on index cards, or place them on your vision board. You can also place them in the Northeast area of your living room, your bedroom, and your office.

Each goal sends your wishes to the Universe, and according to the Law of Attraction, you can attract anything you wish for. Just state your intentions and open yourself up to receive; let the Universe take care of the rest.

If you feel you don't want to place your goals out in the open, you can place them in nice, colored envelopes and address the front to the Universe, God, the Angels, or whomever you are praying to. Remember, Feng Shui is not connected with any specific religion. Instead, it respects all religions and belief systems.

Make your personal Relationship goals even more powerful by adding:

- An image that represents your goal
- An image of someone (such as a celebrity or someone you know personally) who has already attained a similar goal
- Any symbol that represents your goal

For Example:

When you wish to attract spiritual friends, add images of people meditating together, or of several lotuses in a pond.

Special Tip

Single women who want to have a steady romantic relationship should place peonies in their personal relationship direction. They can be real, silk, or just an image. Once you have attracted the relationship you wished for, give the peonies to someone who wishes to have the same kind of luck. Don't keep them. Men can do the same thing but use a bamboo plant instead of peonies.

3/ Quantum Colors for Relationships

In the Quantum Field, the colors for Relationships for Energy Number 7 are **yellow**, **saffron yellow**, and **magenta**. By placing these colors in the Northeast area of your home and office, you are sending a strong signal to the Universe to activate your Relationships.

4/ Relationship Practices

The following are characteristic of those with an Energy Number of 7:

- The most important relationship for you is with God
- You look up to teachers and people who have more knowledge and wisdom than you, and you'll go on to team up with them on a professional level
- Your family and friends will be a source of knowledge and wisdom for you
- Communication and connection on a mental level can be more important to you than on an emotional level
- You may attract partners who are shy and serious
- You'll attract a partner who will be impressed by your knowledge and wisdom
- You need to be able to connect with your partner on a spiritual level
- Meditating, going to church, or praying together are important ways to strengthen your personal relationship
- Your purpose with your partner is to focus on sharing wisdom and knowledge
- You'll enjoy walking together in the mountains
- You'll like to study together, share your passion

about authors, and see each other as students together

- You'll enjoy touching your partner with your hands
- Sometimes you may view sex more like a priest or a monk
- Connect with the power of gemstones and put incense or candles out to create a romantic bedroom
- The colors that stimulate your relationships are rose, pink, fuchsia, yellow, orange, and fire colors like red. Other earth colors like beige, browns, and turquoise are also very stimulating

5/ Feng Shui Activations For Your Relationships in Your Home and Office

1. Facing Direction

Make sure you sit facing, or sleep with your head pointing towards your Relationship direction (Northeast) in order to attract good relationships.

During the day, face the Northeast when you're in the office, attending business meetings, dinners, or important conferences and you will be much more successful with your business relationships.

2. *Activate Your Personal Relationship Direction: Northeast*

To attract better relationships, activate the Northeast area in three places:

- For excellent professional relationships, focus on the Northeast area of your office
- For family relationships, focus on the Northeast area of your family or living room
- To stimulate your personal relationship, focus on the Northeast area of your bedroom

You can use a compass to find the correct direction. Northeast is between 22.5 and 67.5 degrees on a compass. Make sure you are standing facing the foot end of the bed or couch, or sitting down at your desk when you hold the compass. Similarly, you can use the Diamond Compass on the Marie Diamond app that is connected with your Personal Energy Number.

Next, examine the Northeast area of your office, living room, or bedroom. Do the items, furniture, paintings, and colors represent what you wrote down for your Relationship goals?

For example, is an image of a monk walking a lonely road representative of passion with a partner? Make sure there aren't any garbage cans or clutter in the Northeast area because they can block the flow of energy and symbolically put romance and passion "straight into the garbage".

Use objects that you already have in your home to activate your relationship direction. Listed below are several options that will bring good chi to your Relationship energy:

- Square or cubical objects
- Ceramics or crystal objects
- Images and statues of couples, families, Gods, and Goddesses
- Beige, orange, yellow, turquoise, red, rose or purple objects
- Books on relationships
- A picture of a couple praying or meditating together
- An image of a mountain
- Two lotus flowers
- Two candles
- A large rose quartz crystal.
- A large red light
- Two amethyst gemstones

You can also make the space more personal by placing any of the following in your Relationship direction:

- In your office, display a photo of your professional team, or of you and your manager. Also, place your address book or business cards from your clients in the Northeast area
- In your living or family room, display recent photos of you with your loved ones. Also, photos of you and your friends

- In your bedroom, place photos of you with your romantic partner. Photos of you with your children can work here too, but not of you with your mother-in-law

Your Best Direction for <u>Wisdom</u> is <u>West</u>

1/ Soul Journey of Wisdom

Attaining greater wisdom will require you to add more creativity into your spiritual life, such as expressing yourself through dance, painting, or music. To enhance your spiritual awareness, release any emotional problems from your childhood. You will be drawn to teach your children or grandchildren spiritual or religious values. People enjoy listening to your childhood stories.

2/ Goals for Wisdom

Write down your Wisdom goals on index cards, or place them on your vision board. You can also place them in the West area of your living room, your bedroom, and your office.

Each goal sends your wishes to the Universe, and according to the Law of Attraction, you can attract anything you wish for. Just state your intentions and open yourself up to receive; let the Universe take care of the rest.

If you feel you don't want to place your goals out in the open, you can place them in nice, colored envelopes and address the front to the Universe, God, the Angels, or whomever you are praying to. Remember, Feng Shui is not connected with any specific religion. Instead, it respects all religions and belief systems.

Make your personal Wisdom goals even more powerful by adding:

- An image that represents your goal
- An image of someone (such as a celebrity or someone you know personally) who has already attained a similar goal
- Any symbol that represents your goal

For Example:

When you wish to be more joyful in your life, add images of someone who makes you laugh the moment you see their face. Add cartoons or jokes.

3/ Quantum Colors for Wisdom

In the Quantum Field, the colors for Wisdom for Energy Number 7 are **white**, **ivory white**, and **peach**. By placing these colors in the West area of your home and office, you are sending a strong signal to the Universe to activate your Wisdom.

4/ Wisdom Practices

You receive knowledge and wisdom most effectively by:

- Connecting with your inner child
- Releasing your childhood traumas
- Expressing your inner God through dance, music, and painting
- Making mandalas or writing poems to express your soul
- Bringing out your deeply hidden pain
- Seeking therapy
- Accepting your unique qualities
- Laughing and telling jokes
- Gently teasing yourself and not taking yourself too seriously

5/ Feng Shui Activations For Your Wisdom in Your Home and Office

1. Facing Direction

When seeking knowledge or spiritual awareness, sit facing your Wisdom direction (West). It's from the West that your strongest Wisdom energy flows. You will attract greater wisdom and knowledge if you face West whilst you're studying, at your desk, meditating, or praying.

2. Activate Your Personal Wisdom Direction: West

To attract great Wisdom, you need to activate the West areas in three places:

- Stimulate your professional wisdom by placing Feng Shui activations in the West area of your office
- Stimulate your social Wisdom by placing Feng Shui activations in the West of your living or family room
- Stimulate your nightly insights by placing Feng Shui activations in the West of your bedroom

You can use a compass to find the correct direction. West is between 247.5 and 292.5 degrees on a compass. Make sure you are standing facing the foot end of the bed or couch, or sitting down at your desk when you hold the compass. Similarly, you can use the Diamond Compass on the Marie Diamond app that is connected with your Personal Energy Number.

Next, examine the West area of your office, living room, or bedroom. Do the items, furniture, paintings, and colors represent what you wrote down for your Wisdom goals?

For example, an image of a sad little girl shows the Universe you're not letting yourself release the emotional pain from your childhood. Make sure there aren't any garbage cans or clutter in the West area because they can block the flow of energy and symbolically put your Wisdom "straight into the garbage".

Use objects that you already have in your home to activate your Wisdom area. Listed below are several options that will bring good chi to your Wisdom energy:

- Images of white boats sailing on a lake or ocean
- Objects related to the wind, such as flags or windsocks
- Metal wind chimes (six rods with hollow metal tubes are best)
- Gemstones

You can also make the space more personal by placing any of the following in your Wisdom direction:

- In your living room, an image of your church or spiritual community
- In your office, quotes from enlightened businessmen or books on business ethics
- In your bedroom, a bible or any meditation tools

Your Vision Board

When you make a vision board, it helps to think of it as a map. The difference is that at the top of your board always represents the South and the bottom always represents the North. In order to make a vision board that creates the best results with the Law of Attraction, place a photo of you in the center and fill the vision board with the following outline:

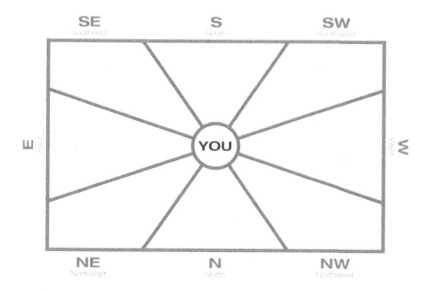

Success Direction

In the bottom, right corner: Northwest
- Write down your Success goals
- Activate it with Success images
- Activate it with the color royal blue and your quantum colors for Success

Health Direction

In the Upper right corner: Southwest
- Write down your Health goals
- Activate it with Health images
- Activate it with the color emerald green and

your quantum colors for Health

Relationship Direction

In the bottom, left corner: Northeast
- Write down your Relationship goals
- Activate it with Relationship images
- Activate it with the color rose and your quantum colors for relationships

Wisdom Direction

In the center on the left: West
- Write down your Wisdom goals
- Activate it with Wisdom images
- Activate it with the color yellow and your quantum colors for Wisdom

The Rest of Your Vision Board

You can fill up the rest of your vision board with images that relate to more general areas of Feng Shui, such as:

- South: Self-esteem, entertainment, dance, enlightenment, and music
- North: Career and journey
- East: Family, health, government, elders, and the past
- Southeast: Money, luxury, and good fortune
- Center: Harmony and balance

Every year, the background colors for the Vision Board change in accordance with the Yearly Law of Attraction based on Diamond Time Feng Shui.

Look for the most current Diamond Vision Board Poster, and for other Marie Diamond Feng Shui products at: http://mariediamond.com

CHAPTER 9
Energy Number 8/5 (Woman):
The Connector

The Information for this Energy Number is the Same as for the Energy Number 5 (Woman)

Introduction

The Energy Archetype connected with Energy Number 8 / 5 (Woman) is called the **Connector**. The essence of the Connector is:

"You nurture others with your talents and gifts. You work best if you're collaborating and teaming up with others. You need others to take care of your creativity, and communication is the bridge in your relationships. Meditating or praying is your natural path for growth."

Famous People With This Energy Number:

Will Smith, Arnold Schwarzenegger, Avril Lavigne, and Ariana Grande

Your Best Direction for <u>Success</u> is <u>Southwest</u>

1/ Soul Journey of Success

Your nurturing qualities will be visible in your career. Taking care of people, business, and your environment is what you do best. You understand the choices of others and try to assist them with compassion.

The greatest lesson the Energy Number 8/ 5 (Woman) needs to learn is to take care of themselves. They tend to think about everyone else more than they think about themselves.

2/ Goals for Success

Affirmations share with the Universe your intention for what it is you want to accomplish in your life. But it's not just a message. There's strength in writing these goals in the present tense; you're not demanding or requesting. You're simply telling the Universe what will be. You should never write your affirmations in the future tense as there is great power in stating "This is the way I want my life to be, here and now".

Write down your Success goals on index cards, or place them on your vision board. You can also place them in the Southwest area of your living room, your bedroom, and your office.

Each goal sends your wishes to the Universe, and according to the Law of Attraction, you can attract anything you wish for. Just state your intentions and open yourself up to receive; let the Universe take care of the rest.

If you feel you don't want to place your goals out in the open, you can place them in nice, colored envelopes and address the front to the Universe, God, the Angels, or whomever you are praying to. Remember, Feng Shui is not connected with any specific religion. Instead, it respects all religions and belief systems.

Make your personal Success goals even more powerful by adding:

- An image that represents your goal
- An image of someone (such as a celebrity or someone you know personally) who has already attained a similar goal
- Any symbol that represents your goal

For Example:

You wish to become a more elegant woman. Add images of famous elegant women and clippings from fashion magazines.

3/ Quantum Colors for Success

In the Quantum Field, the colors for success for the Energy Number 8/ 5 (Woman) are **rose**, **pink**, and **fuchsia**. By placing these colors in the Southwest area of your home and office, you are sending a strong signal to the Universe to activate your Success.

These colors were revealed to me after years of meditation and contemplation, and they are unique to Diamond Feng Shui.

4/ Professional Choices

For you, success and wealth are more likely when you choose the following activities or professional fields:

- A nurse or doctor
- A nanny or a school teacher for children and teenagers
- Real estate agent
- Feng Shui consultant
- Interior designer
- Hostess or hotel manager
- Owner of or working in a restaurant
- Environmentalist or working in an organization that promotes sustainable living
- Residential building contractor
- Gemstone shop owner or diamond cutter
- Women's clothing store owner or fashion designer
- Writer and speaker for women
- Strategic alliances and collaboration
- Networking with women

5/ Feng Shui Activations For Your Success in your Home and Office

1. Facing Direction

During the day, make sure you're facing your Success direction (Southwest) whilst working or meeting up with clients. It's from the Southwest that your strongest Success energy flows. Your ability to attract Success increases greatly when you face towards the Southwest direction whilst you're working, sitting at your desk, looking at your computer screen, when meeting with people, negotiating, and signing contracts.

Avoid sitting with your back to the door since it's poor Feng Shui. From an evolutionary standpoint, our early ancestors faced a lot of dangers in their lives. From wild animals to attacks from other tribes, they had to be completely aware of their surroundings in order to survive.

So, from that viewpoint, it makes sense to have a clear view of your door when you're sitting down or in bed so that you know exactly who's coming into the room. If you can't see the door, you make yourself vulnerable to people sneaking up on you.

In terms of Feng Shui, you want to make sure you're in the path of the incoming flow of positive energy. You want to see all the good opportunities that enter through the door, and you want to make sure you're making yourself accessible to any good fortune that comes knocking.

2. Activate Your Personal Success Direction: Southwest

To attract great success, you need to activate the Southwest area in three places:

- Professional success is focused in the Southwest area of your office
- Personal success is focused in the Southwest area of your living room or family room
- Romantic success is focused in the Southwest area of your bedroom

You can use a compass to find the correct direction. Southwest is between 202.5 and 247.5 degrees on a compass. Make sure you are standing facing the foot end of the bed or couch, or sitting down at your desk when you hold the compass. Similarly, you can use the Diamond Compass on the Marie Diamond app that is connected with your Personal Energy Number.

Next, examine the Southwest area of your office, living room, and bedroom. Do the items, furniture, paintings, and colors represent what you wrote down for your Success goals?

For example, having an image of a ravine can create the feeling that your success is falling into a hole. Make sure there aren't any garbage cans or clutter in the Southwest area because they can block the flow of energy and symbolically put your Success "straight into the garbage".

Use objects that you already have in your home to activate your Success direction.

Listed below are several options that will bring good chi to your Success energy:

- Square or cubical objects
- Ceramics or crystal objects
- Two rose quartz hearts that are touching
- Items grouped together in pairs
- A globe
- The double happiness symbol
- A pair of love birds
- A pair of mandarin ducks connected with a red ribbon
- Images of romantic couples with lasting relationships
- Images of a team playing together and having fun
- A ceramic friendship circle
- Images of compassionate mothers, like Kuan Yin or Lady Mary
- Two red or rose candles
- A citrine gemstone tree

In the office, you can also make the space more personal by placing any of the following in your Success direction:

- The logo of your company
- Your products or designs
- Your vision board with your goals
- A personal success affirmation card
- The royal blue Yin Yang symbol

Your Best Direction For <u>Health</u> is <u>Northwest</u>

1/ Soul Journey of Health

Just as you like to take care of others, you also need to be open to others taking care of you. Take time to relax and get a massage. Do something with your hands to keep your whole body healthy. Meditation and prayer time will improve your emotional and mental health.

2/ Goals for Health

Write down your Health goals on index cards, or place them on your vision board. You can also place them in the Northwest area of your living room, your bedroom, and your office.

Each goal sends your wishes to the Universe, and according to the Law of Attraction, you can attract anything you wish for. Just state your intentions and open yourself up to receive; let the Universe take care of the rest.

If you feel you don't want to place your goals out in the open, you can place them in nice, colored envelopes and address the front to the Universe, God, the Angels, or whomever you are praying to. Remember, Feng Shui is not connected with any specific religion. Instead, it respects all religions and belief systems.

Make your personal Health goals even more powerful by adding:

- An image that represents your goal
- An image of someone (such as a celebrity or someone you know personally) who has already attained a similar goal
- Any symbol that represents your goal

For Example:

You wish to give and receive many massages. Add images of someone being massaged and clippings from magazines or books on the topic.

3/ Quantum Colors for Health

In the Quantum Field, the colors for Health for the Energy Number 8/ 5 (Woman) are **opal**, **diamond**, and **silver**. By placing these colors in the Northwest of your home and office, you are sending a strong signal to the Universe to activate your Health.

4/ Health Practices

The following suggestions can help enhance your health energy. These suggestions will not guarantee your health, but instead will make it easier for you to become healthier:

- Take extra care of your head
- Have massages with gentle oils
- Go to a chiropractor
- Find peace in your hobbies and passions
- Don't display images of people carrying things on their head
- Display images of hands or of an open hand
- Manicures are very relaxing for you
- Take time to relax and connect with God or the Universe
- Spend time with your friends
- Colors that stimulate your health are gold, silver, white and earth tones like beige, yellow, and orange
- Surround yourself with gemstones
- Go on a trip to the mountains or a desert where you can see the sky and gaze at the stars
- Release emotional issues with your father
- Keep a positive attitude with your manager
- Don't focus too much on other people's problems

5/ Feng Shui Activations For Your Health in Your Home and Office

1. Facing your Direction

When you're in bed, sleep with the top of your head pointing toward your Health direction (Northwest). During the day, sit in your living space or in your dining room facing your health direction.

Your energy level will increase when you sleep with the crown of your head pointing toward this direction, so arrange your bed so you can do so. If you lie on your couch when you're ill, make sure the top of your head faces the Northwest.

2. Activate Your Personal Health Direction: Northwest

To attract good health, you need to activate the Northwest in three places:

- To stimulate your energy for health when you're working, place Feng Shui activations in the Northwest area of your office. A healthy worker creates a healthy business
- Place Feng Shui activations in the Northwest of your living or family room so that during the daytime, you're creating good energy
- Place Feng Shui activations in the Northwest of your bedroom to stimulate your health whilst you're sleeping and to help you wake up energized in the morning

You can use a compass to find the correct direction. Northwest is between 292.5 and 337.5 degrees on a compass. Make sure you are standing facing the foot end of the bed or couch, or sitting down at your desk when you hold the compass. Similarly, you can use the Diamond Compass on the Marie Diamond app that is connected with your Personal Energy Number.

Next, examine the Northwest area of your office, living room, or bedroom. Do the items, furniture, paintings, and colors represent what you wrote down for your Health goals?

For example, a painting of someone walking totally exhausted in the desert, looking for water, will be a drain on your health. Make sure there aren't any garbage cans or clutter in the Northwest area because they can block the flow of energy and symbolically put your Health "straight into the garbage".

Use objects that you already have in your home to activate your Health direction. Listed below are several options that will bring good chi to your Health energy:

- Round or oval objects
- Metal or metal-colored objects
- Images of stars, moons, and planets
- Images of wise men like Einstein
- Images of Saints, Angels, or spiritual and religious leaders
- White or gray objects
- Ceramics or crystal objects
- Images of Prophets like Jesus or Buddha or Holy Men
- Metal wind chimes (six rod with hollow metal tubes are best)
- Gemstones
- A Wu Lou

You can also make the space more personal by placing any of the following in your Health direction:

- An image of yourself when you appeared radiant and healthy in your living room
- Your vitamins, food supplements, workout or exercise equipment in your bedroom
- Books on health, yoga or relaxation in your office

Your Best Direction for <u>Relationships</u> is <u>West</u>

1/ Soul Journey of Relationships

You love to connect with joyful and creative people. Children and grandchildren are the treasures of your life. You attract artists and spontaneous people as friends and as partners. You want deep connection with others, not superficial relationships. You're sometimes too spontaneous and promise things to people too quickly because you want to please them. You're innocent but sometimes to the point of being naïve in trusting everyone you meet.

2/ Goals for Relationships

Write down your Relationship goals on index cards, or place them on your vision board. You can also place them in the West area of your living room, your bedroom, and your office.

Each goal sends your wishes to the Universe, and according to the Law of Attraction, you can attract anything you wish for. Just state your intentions and open yourself up to receive; let the Universe take care of the rest.

If you feel you don't want to place your goals out in the open, you can place them in nice, colored envelopes and address the front to the Universe, God, the Angels, or whomever you are praying to. Remember, Feng Shui is not connected with any specific religion. Instead, it respects all religions and belief systems.

Make your personal Relationship goals even more powerful by adding:

- An image that represents your goal
- An image of someone (such as a celebrity or someone you know personally) who has already attained a similar goal
- Any symbol that represents your goal

For Example:

You wish to have more children in your life. Add images of you surrounded with children playing a game together.

Special Tip

Single women who want to have a steady romantic relationship should place peonies in their personal relationship direction. They can be real, silk, or just an image. Once you have attracted the relationship you wished for, give the peonies to someone who wishes to have the same kind of luck. Don't keep them. Men can do the same thing but use a bamboo plant instead of peonies.

3/ Quantum Colors for Relationships

In the Quantum Field, the colors for Relationships for Energy Number 8/ 5 (Woman) are **white**, **ivory white**, and **peach**. By placing these colors in the West area of your home and office, you are sending a strong signal to the Universe to activate your Relationships.

4/ Relationship Practices

The following are characteristic of those with an Energy Number of 8/ 5 (Woman):

- You love playing with children or grandchildren
- Children trust you as you're in touch with your inner child
- You attract youthful romantic partners; they could be younger than you or they just have a youthful look and act very spontaneous
- You like to be creative with your friends
- You have artists and musicians as partners or

friends
- You like to have deep conversations about life
- You love to walk by the ocean or lake with your loved one
- You love calmness and peace in relationships
- You avoid conflicts and would rather give in to other people's conditions
- You are naive and innocent in relationships
- You are full of wonder and open to new, creative ideas in relationships

5/ Feng Shui Activations For Your Relationships in Your Home and Office

1. Facing Direction

Make sure you sit facing, or sleep with your head pointing towards your Relationship direction (West) in order to attract good relationships.

During the day, face the West when you're in the office, attending business meetings, dinners, or important conferences and you will be much more successful with your business relationships.

2. Activate Your Personal Relationship Direction: West

To attract better relationships, activate the West area in three places:

- For excellent professional relationships, focus on the West area of your office
- For family relationships, focus on the West area of your family or living room
- To stimulate your personal relationship, focus on the West area of your bedroom

You can use a compass to find the correct direction. West is between 247.5 and 292.5 degrees on a compass. Make sure you are standing facing the foot end of the bed or couch, or sitting down at your desk when you hold the compass. Similarly, you can use the Diamond Compass on the Marie Diamond app that is connected with your Personal Energy Number.

Next, examine the West area of your office, living room, or bedroom. Do the items, furniture, paintings, and colors represent what you wrote down for your Relationship goals?

For example, if you have images of old people don't be surprised if you are not having a great relationship with your children. Make sure there aren't any garbage cans or clutter in the West area because they can block the flow of energy and symbolically put romance and passion "straight into the garbage".

Use objects that you already have in your home to activate your relationship direction.

Listed below are several options that will bring good chi to your Relationship energy:

- Round or oval objects
- Metal or metal-colored object
- Artwork or crafts
- Playful objects, toys, and gadgets
- White or gray objects
- Ceramics or crystal objects
- Crystal heart
- Pictures of children playing
- Images of a lake or ocean with white boats sailing on it
- Objects connected with the wind, like flags
- Gemstones
- Metal wind chimes

You can also make the space more personal by placing any of the following in your Relationship direction:

- In your office, display a photo of your professional team, or of you and your manager. Also, place your address book or business cards from your clients in the West area
- In your living or family room, display recent photos of you with your loved ones. Also, photos of you and your friends
- In your bedroom, place photos of you with your romantic partner. Photos of you with your children can work here too, but not of you with your mother-in-law

Your Best Direction for <u>Wisdom</u> is <u>Northeast</u>

1/ Soul Journey of Wisdom

You gain wisdom by studying the ancient teachers and books. Reading biographies of people that inspire you in your professional field will be helpful.

Traveling to the mountains and taking time to meditate, walk, or ski will inspire you. Learn how to follow your intuition and your inner guidance. Connect with beings of light from other realms like masters, guides, and angels.

2/ Goals for Wisdom

Write down your Wisdom goals on index cards, or place them on your vision board. You can also place them in the Northeast area of your living room, your bedroom, and your office.

Each goal sends your wishes to the Universe, and according to the Law of Attraction, you can attract anything you wish for. Just state your intentions and open yourself up to receive; let the Universe take care of the rest.

If you feel you don't want to place your goals out in the open, you can place them in nice, colored envelopes and address the front to the Universe, God, the Angels, or whomever you are praying to. Remember, Feng Shui is not connected with any specific religion. Instead, it respects all religions and belief systems.

Make your personal Wisdom goals even more powerful by adding:

- An image that represents your goal
- An image of someone (such as a celebrity or someone you know personally) who has already attained a similar goal
- Any symbol that represents your goal

For Example:

You wish to have more time to connect with God. Add images of someone who is praying. You can add images of a spiritual or religious leader who is an example of devotion.

3/ Quantum Colors for Wisdom

In the Quantum Field, the colors for Wisdom for Energy Number 8/ 5 (Woman) are **yellow**, **saffron yellow**, and **magenta**.

By placing these colors in the Northeast area of your home and office, you are sending a strong signal to the Universe to activate your Wisdom.

4/ Wisdom Practices

You receive knowledge and wisdom most effectively by:

- You are a natural teacher on any subject
- You love to pray and meditate
- You'll be attracted to very wise and spiritual people
- From a young age, your connection with God will be a part of your life
- You love to be in temples, churches, or places in nature where you feel spiritual power
- You love to study the bible or other religious texts
- You are devoted to your church, your religion, your teacher or master
- You love to be on top of a mountain
- You will have many spiritual or religious items and images in your home
- You have a religious or spiritual altar
- You collect books
- Reading is your way of relaxing and getting inspiration

5/ Feng Shui Activations For Your Wisdom in Your Home and Office

1. Facing Direction

When seeking knowledge or spiritual awareness, sit facing your Wisdom direction (Northeast). It's from the Northeast that your strongest Wisdom energy flows. You will attract greater wisdom and knowledge if you face the Northeast whilst you're studying, at your desk, meditating, or praying.

2. Activate Your Personal Wisdom Direction: Northeast

To attract great Wisdom, you need to activate the Northeast areas in three places:

- Stimulate your professional wisdom by placing Feng Shui activations in the Northeast area of your office
- Stimulate your social Wisdom by placing Feng Shui activations in the Northeast of your living or family room
- Stimulate your nightly insights by placing Feng Shui activations in the Northeast of your bedroom

You can use a compass to find the correct direction. Northeast is between 22.5 and 67.5 degrees on a compass. Make sure you are standing facing the foot end of the bed or couch, or sitting down at your desk when you hold the compass. Similarly, you can use the Diamond Compass on the Marie Diamond app that is connected with your Personal Energy Number.

Next, examine the Northeast area of your office, living room, or bedroom. Do the items, furniture, paintings, and colors represent what you wrote down for your

Wisdom goals?

For example, you have an image or a statue of someone sitting with his head between his hands looking down and depressed. Do you think this depressed man is open to God and the Universe? Make sure there aren't any garbage cans or clutter in the Northeast area because they can block the flow of energy and symbolically put your Wisdom "straight into the garbage".

Use objects that you already have in your home to activate your Wisdom area. Listed below are several options that will bring good chi to your Wisdom energy:

- Square or cubical objects
- Ceramics or crystal objects
- Images and statues of praying or meditating saints
- Beige, orange, yellow, turquoise, red, rose, or purple objects
- Books on spirituality and religion
- Your awards and certificates
- Images of a mountain (but not one totally covered with snow)
- One lotus flower
- One candle
- One large red light
- Amethyst gemstones

You can also make the space more personal by placing any of the following in your Wisdom direction:

- In your living room, an image of your church or spiritual community.
- In your office, quotes from enlightened businessmen or books on business ethics
- In your bedroom, a bible or any meditation tools

Your Vision Board

When you make a vision board, it helps to think of it as a map. The difference is that at the top of your board always represents the South and the bottom always represents the North. In order to make a vision board that creates the best results with the Law of Attraction, place a photo of you in the center and fill the vision board with the following outline:

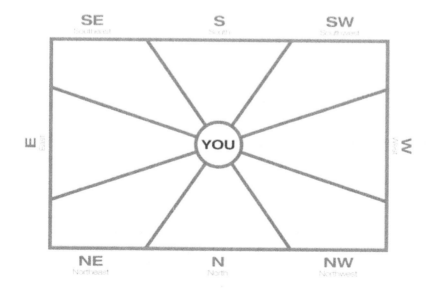

Your Success Direction

In the upper right corner: Southwest
- Write down your Success goals
- Activate it with Success images
- Activate it with the color royal blue and your quantum colors for Success

Your Health Direction

In the bottom, right corner: Northwest
- Write down your Health goals
- Activate it with Health images
- Activate it with the color emerald green and your quantum colors for Health

Your Relationship Direction

In the center right area: West
- Write down your Relationship goals
- Activate it with Relationship images
- Activate it with the color rose and your quantum colors for relationships

Your Wisdom Direction

In the bottom left corner: Northeast
- Write down your Wisdom goals
- Activate it with Wisdom images
- Activate it with the color yellow and your quantum colors for Wisdom

The Rest of Your Vision Board

You can fill up the rest of your vision board with images that relate to more general areas of Feng Shui, such as:

- South: Self-esteem, entertainment, dance enlightenment, and music
- North: Career and journey
- East: Family, health, government, elders, and the past
- Southeast: Money, luxury, and good fortune
- Center: Harmony and balance

Every year, the background colors for the Vision Board change in accordance with the Yearly Law of Attraction based on Diamond Time Feng Shui.

Look for the most current Diamond Vision Board Poster, and for other Marie Diamond Feng Shui products at: http://mariediamond.com

CHAPTER 10
Energy Number 9:
The Healer

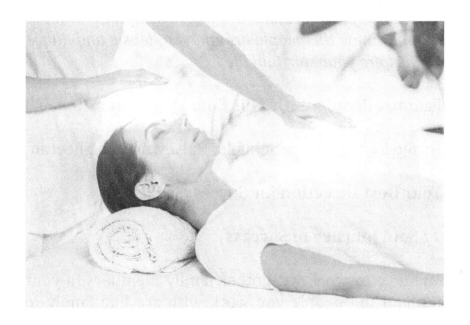

Introduction

The Energy Archetype connected with Energy Number 9 is called the **Healer.** The essence of the Healer is:

"You're open to new ideas, new possibilities, and perspectives. Money can create stress on your health so make sure your accounts are in order. Don't become a hermit. Enjoy the people around you. Music and dance will inspire your spiritual life."

Famous People With This Energy Number:

Nicole Kidman, Jerry Seinfeld, Halsey, and Ed Sheeran

Your Best Direction for <u>Success</u> is <u>East</u>

1/ Soul Journey of Success

You love to work with other family members in your job and the people you work with are like family to you. Having time with your family is your ultimate purpose. You can be successful inventing new instruments and new tools for the body, mind, and soul. You enjoy working in historical buildings or with ancient traditions.

You're here to bridge the past with the future. Just make sure you take time to enjoy nature and to avoid working all the time. Your real passions need to become visible.

2/ Goals for Success

Affirmations share with the Universe your intention for what it is you want to accomplish in your life. But it's not just a message. There's strength in writing these goals in the present tense; you're not demanding or requesting. You're simply telling the Universe what will be. You should never write your affirmations in the future tense as there is great power in stating "This is the way I want my life to be, here and now".

Write down your Success goals on index cards, or place them on your vision board. You can also place them in the East area of your living room, your bedroom, and your office.

Each goal sends your wishes to the Universe, and according to the Law of Attraction, you can attract anything you wish for. Just state your intentions and open yourself up to receive; let the Universe take care of the rest.

If you feel you don't want to place your goals out in the open, you can place them in nice, colored envelopes and address the front to the Universe, God, the Angels, or whomever you are praying to. Remember, Feng Shui is not connected with any specific religion. Instead, it respects all religions and belief systems.

Make your personal Success goals even more powerful by adding:

- An image that represents your goal
- An image of someone (such as a celebrity or someone you know personally) who has already attained a similar goal
- Any symbol that represents your goal

For Example:

You want to connect more with local environmental groups. Place some of their projects in your success area.

3/ Quantum Colors for Success

In the Quantum Field, the colors for Success for the Energy Number 9 are **emerald green**, **citrus green**, and **iris blue**. By placing these colors in the East area of your home and office, you are sending a strong signal to the Universe to activate your Success.

These colors were revealed to me after years of meditation and contemplation, and they are unique to Diamond Feng Shui.

4/ Professional Choices

For you, success and wealth are more likely when you choose the following activities or professional fields:

- Working in the family business
- Secondhand bookseller
- Producer of musical instruments
- Gardener or florist
- Historian
- Independent investor
- Wood craft sales
- Government work
- Police officer
- Insurance industry
- Stay-at-home parent
- Environmental activist
- Biologist
- Musician
- Healer

5/ Feng Shui Activations For Your Success in your Home and Office

1. Facing Direction

During the day, make sure you're facing your Success direction (East) whilst working or meeting up with clients. It's from the East that your strongest Success energy flows. Your ability to attract Success increases greatly when you face towards the East whilst you're working, sitting at your desk, looking at your computer screen, when meeting with people, negotiating, and signing contracts.

Avoid sitting with your back to the door since it's poor Feng Shui. From an evolutionary standpoint, our early ancestors faced a lot of dangers in their lives. From wild animals to attacks from other tribes, they had to be completely aware of their surroundings in order to survive. So, from that viewpoint, it makes sense to have a clear view of your door when you're sitting down or in bed so that you know exactly who's coming into the room. If you can't see the door, you make yourself vulnerable to people sneaking up on you.

In terms of Feng Shui, you want to make sure you're in the path of the incoming flow of positive energy. You want to see all the good opportunities that enter through the door, and you want to make sure you're making yourself accessible to any good fortune that comes knocking.

2. Activate Your Personal Success Direction: East

To attract great Success, you need to activate the East area in three places:

- Professional success is focused in the East area of your office
- Personal success is focused in the East area of your living room or family room
- Romantic success is focused in the East area of your bedroom

You can use a compass to find the correct direction. East is between 67.5 and 112.5 degrees on a compass. Make sure you are standing facing the foot end of the bed or couch, or sitting down at your desk when you hold the compass. Similarly, you can use the Diamond Compass on the Marie Diamond app that is connected with your Personal Energy Number.

Next, examine the East area of your office, living room, and bedroom. Do the items, furniture, paintings, and colors represent what you wrote down for your Success goals?

For example, having an image of a wrecked ship represents a sinking career. Make sure there aren't any garbage cans or clutter in the East area because they can block the flow of energy and symbolically put your Success "straight into the garbage".

Use objects that you already have in your home to activate your Success direction. Listed below are several options that will bring good chi to your Success energy:

- Long and tall objects and objects with stripes
- Wooden and glass objects
- Antiques
- Flowers and plants
- Images of flowers, plants, forest and gardens
- Brown and green objects
- Pictures of elders
- An image of a river or a fountain
- Bamboo wind chimes
- Jade or aventurine gemstone tree

In the office, you can also make the space more personal by placing any of the following in your Success direction:

- The logo of your company
- Your products or designs
- Your vision board with your goals
- A personal success affirmation card

Your Best Direction for <u>Health</u> is <u>Southeast</u>

1/ Soul Journey of Health

Your health is your great fortune. Always take special care of your skeletal structure. Visit your osteopath or chiropractor regularly. Your health is challenged by too much stress about your finances. Playing golf is great for your health because being in nature and handling the long golf club is stimulating to you. Walking in nature is also great for you.

2/ Goals for Health

Write down your Health goals on index cards, or place them on your vision board. You can also place them in the Southeast area of your living room, your bedroom, and your office.

Each goal sends your wishes to the Universe, and according to the Law of Attraction, you can attract anything you wish for. Just state your intentions and open yourself up to receive; let the Universe take care of the rest.

If you feel you don't want to place your goals out in the open, you can place them in nice, colored envelopes and address the front to the Universe, God, the Angels, or whomever you are praying to. Remember, Feng Shui is not connected with any specific religion. Instead, it respects all religions and belief systems.

Make your personal Health goals even more powerful by adding:

- An image that represents your goal
- An image of someone (such as a celebrity or someone you know personally) who has already attained a similar goal
- Any symbol that represents your goal

For Example:

You want to find the best osteopath for your health. Place the list of all Osteopaths in your area in your health direction.

3/ Quantum Colors for Health

In the Quantum Field, the colors for Health for the Energy Number 9 are **violet**, **lilac**, and **gold**. By placing these colors in the Southeast area of your home and office, you are sending a strong signal to the Universe to activate your Health.

4/ Health Practices

The following suggestions can help enhance your health energy. These suggestions will not guarantee your health, but instead will make it easier for you to become healthier.

- Play golf
- Go for walks in nature
- Eat foods that help prevent osteoporosis
- Visit an osteopath or chiropractor
- Learn ballet or dance
- Wear beneficial colors such as green and brown
- Don't keep any dried flowers in your living space
- Water your plants regularly
- Release past experiences
- Forgive yourself for anything you have held on to from the past
- Let others help you manage finances
- Make sure your accounts are in order
- Pay your bills on time
- Take good care of your wallet
- Display an image of a healthy millionaire or someone who made their millions with great health products
- Spend money on good health care and practitioners

5/ Feng Shui Activations For Your Health in Your Home and Office

1. Facing Direction

When you're in bed, sleep with the top of your head pointing toward your Health direction (Southeast). During the day, sit in your living space or in your dining room facing your health direction.

Your energy level will increase when you sleep with the crown of your head pointing toward this direction, so arrange your bed so you can do so. If you lie on your couch when you're ill, make sure the top of your head faces the Southeast.

2. Activate Your Personal Health Direction: Southeast

To attract good Health, you need to activate the Southeast in three places:

- To stimulate your energy for health when you're working, place Feng Shui activations in the Southeast area of your office. A healthy worker creates a healthy business
- Place Feng Shui activations in the Southeast of your living or family room so that during the daytime, you're creating good energy
- Place Feng Shui activations in the Southeast of your bedroom to stimulate your health whilst you're sleeping and to help you wake up

energized in the morning

You can use a compass to find the correct direction. Southeast is between 112.5 and 157.5 degrees on a compass. Make sure you are standing facing the foot end of the bed or couch, or sitting down at your desk when you hold the compass. Similarly, you can use the Diamond Compass on the Marie Diamond app that is connected with your Personal Energy Number.

Next, examine the Southeast area of your office, living room, or bedroom. Do the items, furniture, paintings, and colors represent what you wrote down for your Health goals?

For example, dead flowers in the Southeast can attract problems with your immune system. Make sure there aren't any garbage cans or clutter in the Southeast area because they can block the flow of energy and symbolically put your Health "straight into the garbage".

Use objects that you already have in your home to activate your Health direction. Listed below are several options that will bring good chi to your Health energy:

- Cylinder-shaped objects, objects with stripes, or long and tall objects
- Objects made of wood
- Images of flowers and plants (but don't use plants with spiky leaves like cacti, palm trees, or

yuccas, because they create attacking energy in your living space)

- Real flowers and plants (again, no spiky leaves because they pick away at your success)
- Silk flowers and plastic plants (but not dried flowers)
- Brown, beige, green, and lilac colored objects
- Magazines and books on financial advice or creating wealth and money
- A wealth ship, a money frog or a bowl with coins
- Images of millionaires and billionaires
- A small fountain
- An image of a small waterfall, a river in a green lush landscape, or a bamboo plant

You can also make the space more personal by placing any of the following in your Health direction:

- An image of yourself when you appeared radiant and healthy in your living room
- Your vitamins, food supplements, workout or exercise equipment in your bedroom
- Books on health, yoga or relaxation in your office

Your Best Direction For <u>Relationships</u> is <u>North</u>

1/ Soul Journey of Relationships

Loneliness may be a part of who you are. Even in a relationship, you may still find yourself feeling alone and as though people don't understand you. Walking with your partner and friends at the beach will help you communicate. Enjoy days at the spa together with your partner too to relax and feel romantic. You need to have a romantic partner who can understand your professional ambition and who walks the ambitious road with you.

2/ Goals for Relationships

Write down your Relationship goals on index cards, or place them on your vision board. You can also place them in the North area of your living room, your bedroom, and your office.

Each goal sends your wishes to the Universe, and according to the Law of Attraction, you can attract anything you wish for. Just state your intentions and open yourself up to receive; let the Universe take care of the rest.

If you feel you don't want to place your goals out in the open, you can place them in nice, colored envelopes and address the front to the Universe, God, the Angels, or whomever you are praying to. Remember, Feng Shui is not connected with any specific religion. Instead, it respects all religions and belief systems.

Make your personal Relationship goals even more powerful by adding:

- An image that represents your goal
- An image of someone (such as a celebrity or someone you know personally) who has already attained a similar goal
- Any symbol that represents your goal

For Example:

You want to work closely with your future partner. You can place images of a couple working together in harmony.

Special Tip

Single women who want to have a steady romantic relationship should place peonies in their personal relationship direction. They can be real, silk, or just an image.

Once you have attracted the relationship you wished for, give the peonies to someone who wishes to have the same kind of luck. Don't keep them. Men can do the same thing but use a bamboo plant instead of peonies.

3/ Quantum Colors for Relationships

In the Quantum Field, the colors for Relationships for Energy Number 9 are **royal blue**, **cobalt blue**, and **aqua blue.** By placing these colors in the North area of your home and office, you are sending a strong signal to the Universe to activate your Relationships.

4/ Relationship Practices

The following are characteristic of those with an Energy Number of 9:

- It may take you a long time to find your great romantic partner. It may come for you at a later age.
- You have high standards and want a partner who is perfect in your eyes
- When you marry, you want a lifetime commitment
- You're more likely to attract a partner who shares your professional field and who you can fall in love with at work
- Working together with your partner is very important for you
- You want a partner whose income helps support the family
- You love to stay busy and enjoy doing projects together around the home
- You love to know all the future projects of your partner and family

- You love walking or cycling with your friends, family, and loved ones

5/ Feng Shui Activations For Your Relationships in Your Home and Office

1. Facing Direction

Make sure you sit facing, or sleep with your head pointing towards your relationship direction (North) in order to attract good relationships.

During the day, face the North when you're in the office, attending business meetings, dinners, or important conferences and you will be much more successful with your business relationships.

2. Activate Your Personal Relationship Direction: North

To attract better relationships, activate the North area in three places:

- For excellent professional relationships, focus on the North area of your office
- For family relationships, focus on the North area of your family or living room
- To stimulate your personal relationship, focus on the North area of your bedroom

You can use a compass to find the correct direction. North is between 337.5 and 22.5 degrees on a compass. Make sure you are standing facing the foot end of the bed or couch, or sitting down at your desk when you hold the compass. Similarly, you can use the Diamond Compass on the Marie Diamond app that is connected with your Personal Energy Number.

Next, examine the North area of your office, living room, or bedroom. Do the items, furniture, paintings, and colors represent what you wrote down for your Relationship goals?

For example, an image of two strangers on a bench does not represent your ideal personal relationship. Make sure there aren't any garbage cans or clutter in the North area because they can block the flow of energy and symbolically put romance and passion "straight into the garbage".

Use objects that you already have in your home to activate your Relationship direction. Listed below are several options that will bring good chi to your Relationship energy:

- Irregular or asymmetric objects
- Glass or transparent objects
- A fountain or an aquarium
- Images of a river or a waterfall
- Blue or black items
- An image of a road
- An image of a white sailboat
- A golden double happiness symbol

You can also make the space more personal by placing any of the following in your Relationship direction:

- In your office, display a photo of your professional team, or of you and your manager. Also, place your address book or business cards from your clients in the North area
- In your living or family room, display recent photos of you with your loved ones. Also, photos of you and your friends
- In your bedroom, place photos of you with your romantic partner. Photos of you with your children can work here too, but not of you with your mother-in-law

Your Best Direction for Wisdom is South

1/ Soul Journey of Wisdom

Your spiritual or religious life can be best expressed by singing and dancing. Gratitude for life will be part of your spiritual journey. Self-esteem seminars are great for you. You need to learn that you don't have to be so dependent on external sources. You can believe and accept your inner voice, and accept the power of the God/the Universe within.

2/ Goals for Wisdom

Write down your Wisdom goals on index cards, or place them on your vision board. You can also place them in the South area of your living room, your bedroom, and your office.

Each goal sends your wishes to the Universe, and according to the Law of Attraction, you can attract anything you wish for. Just state your intentions and open yourself up to receive; let the Universe take care of the rest.

If you feel you don't want to place your goals out in the open, you can place them in nice, colored envelopes and address the front to the Universe, God, the Angels, or whomever you are praying to. Remember, Feng Shui is not connected with any specific religion. Instead, it respects all religions and belief systems.

Make your personal Wisdom goals even more powerful by adding:

- An image that represents your goal
- An image of someone (such as a celebrity or someone you know personally) who has already attained a similar goal
- Any symbol that represents your goal

For Example:

You wish to celebrate God in your family. Add images of a family going to church and singing together.

3/ Quantum Colors for Wisdom

In the Quantum Field, the colors for Wisdom for Energy Number 9 are **ruby red**, **cherry red**, and **orange**. By placing these colors in the South area of your home and office, you are sending a strong signal to the Universe to activate your Wisdom.

4/ Wisdom Practices

You receive knowledge and wisdom most effectively by:

- Singing in a choir
- Dancing from your soul
- Expressing your creativity with the grace of God
- Attending self-esteem seminars
- Praying to Saints and devoting yourself to a Master
- Following your passion
- Sitting in the sunshine
- Connecting with shamans
- Chanting

5/ Feng Shui Activations For Your Wisdom in Your Home and Office

1. Facing Direction

When seeking knowledge or spiritual awareness, sit facing your Wisdom direction (South). It's from the South that your strongest Wisdom energy flows. You will attract greater wisdom and knowledge if you face the South whilst you're studying, at your desk, meditating, or praying.

2. Activate Your Personal Wisdom Direction: South

To attract great Wisdom, you need to activate the South areas in three places:

- Stimulate your professional wisdom by placing Feng Shui activations in the South area of your office
- Stimulate your social Wisdom by placing Feng Shui activations in the South of your living or family room
- Stimulate your nightly insights by placing Feng Shui activations in the South of your bedroom

You can use a compass to find the correct direction. South is between 157.5 and 202.5 degrees on a compass. Make sure you are standing facing the foot end of the bed or couch, or sitting down at your desk when you hold the compass. Similarly, you can use the Diamond Compass on the Marie Diamond app that is connected with your Personal Energy Number.

Next, examine the South area of your office, living room, or bedroom. Do the items, furniture, paintings, and colors represent what you wrote down for your Wisdom goals?

For example, a frozen landscape will not create a great connection with God. Make sure there aren't any garbage cans or clutter in the South area because they can block the flow of energy and symbolically put your Wisdom "straight into the garbage".

Use objects that you already have in your home to activate your wisdom area. Listed below are several options that will bring good chi to your Wisdom energy:

- Triangle or pyramid objects, objects with stripes, or long and tall objects
- Plastic or wooden objects
- Images of flowers and plants (but not spiky leaves like cacti, palm trees, or yuccas because they create attacking energy in your living space)
- Real flowers and plants (again, don't use plants with spiky leaves. You can use silk flowers and plastic plants but not dried flowers)
- Candles or a red lamp
- Images of famous musicians, dancers, and singers
- Images of a temple
- Fire colors like red, purple, yellow, orange, rose, fuchsia, brown, beige, or green colored objects
- Magazines and books about show business, art, or music

You can also make the space more personal by placing any of the following in your Wisdom direction:

- In your living room, an image of your church or spiritual community
- In your office, quotes from enlightened businessmen or books on business ethics
- In your bedroom, a bible or any meditation tools

Your Vision Board

When you make a vision board, it helps to think of it as a map. The difference is that at the top of your board always represents the South and the bottom always represents the North. In order to make a vision board that creates the best results with the Law of Attraction, place a photo of you in the center and fill the vision board with the following outline:

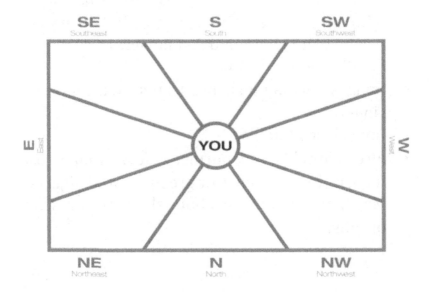

Your Success Direction

In the middle left area: East
- Write down your Success goals
- Activate it with Success images
- Activate it with the color royal blue and your quantum colors for Success

Your Health Direction

In the upper left corner: Southeast
- Write down your Health goals
- Activate it with Health images
- Activate it with the color emerald green and your quantum colors for Health

Your Relationship Direction

In the center of the bottom area: North
- Write down your Relationship goals
- Activate it with Relationship images
- Activate it with the color rose and your quantum colors for relationships

Your Wisdom Direction

In the center on the top: South
- Write down your Wisdom goals
- Activate it with Wisdom images
- Activate it with the color yellow and your quantum colors for Wisdom

The Rest of Your Vision Board

You can fill up the rest of your vision board with images that relate to more general areas of Feng Shui, such as:

- Southwest: Romance, female energy, motherhood, and collaboration
- West: Creativity, children, technology, and communication
- Northwest: Travel, advisors, friends, and space
- Northeast: Wisdom, spirituality, knowledge, and teachers
- Center: Harmony and balance

Every year, the background colors for the Vision Board change in accordance with the Yearly Law of Attraction based on Diamond Time Feng Shui.

Look for the most current Diamond Vision Board Poster, and for other Marie Diamond Feng Shui products at: http://mariediamond.com

Conclusion

I hope that by reading this book, you have been able to gain a deeper understanding of yourself. It's my hope that this new knowledge will inspire you to take action to transform your success, health, relationships, and wisdom.

Keep This Book Close to You

Each time you move to a new house or apartment, or start working in another office, use this book to activate your new surroundings. Each time a friend or family member comes to you with problems about their health or relationships, take this book and share some tips to activate their life.

Share the Results With Others

The next step after practicing and enjoying the results of your newfound wisdom is to share it with others. Share the changes you made to your home and what occurred in your life with others. Buy this book as a gift and help your loved ones transform their own lives.

With Love
Marie Diamond

About the Author

Marie Diamond is a globally renowned Transformational Leader and star of the worldwide phenomenon "The Secret". She uses her extraordinary knowledge of quantum physics, the Law of Attraction, and Feng Shui to help people transform their lives. Her vision is to enlighten more than 500 million people during her lifetime.

Her clients include A-list celebrities in film and music (such as Steven Spielberg, Big Sean, Jason Bateman and Jodie Foster) and top-selling authors and speakers (such as Rhonda Byrne, Jack Canfield, John Gray, the late Bob Proctor, Marianne Williamson and Vishen Lakhiani). She has also advised leaders from Fortune 500 companies, sports athletes, governments, and royal families. Marie Diamond combines her intuitive gifts, the growing science of energy flow, ancient wisdom, and modern tools to enlighten homes, businesses, and people. She is known for her passion to help create enlightened leaders around the world.

She is a founding member of the Transformational Leadership Council, created by Jack Canfield, and President of the Association of Transformational Leaders in Europe. She has more than one million online and in-person students in more than 190 countries. You can connect with her for personal mentoring, consultations, seminars, online courses, eBooks, and home study courses at www.MarieDiamond.com. Her Spanish students can join her at www.MarieDiamondespanol.com. Her teachings are published in online programs such as Mind Valley, Learning Strategies and YouUnity. For her charity work, she is a knighted Dame.

Currently, she lives between the south of France, London, and the USA with her family and her dogs.

Made in United States
North Haven, CT
18 January 2025

64605304R00134